I thought the
Google part might
be useful.
Margaret

A Weekend of Genealogy:
Things to Know and Do Online and Offline

by Margaret M. McMahon, Ph.D.

Copyright © 2014 by Dr. Margaret M. McMahon. All rights reserved. No part of this may be reproduced in any manner whatsoever without written permission, except in the case of brief quotations in articles and reviews. All trademarks or copyrights mentioned herein are the possession of their respective owners and the author makes no claim of ownership my mention of products that contain these marks. Cover photo ©Will O' The Wrist.

Disclaimer

The author has no commercial connection with any of the trademark holders.

All rights reserved.

ISBN: 1500584681
ISBN-13: 978-1500584689

DEDICATION

I am always grateful for the two guys who support all my endeavors, the Michaels. It has been a great year of hard work and change for all of us, mostly for the better. I would never have predicted that a descendant of Irish immigrants would be living with two Pilgrims.

CONTENTS

ACKNOWLEDGMENTS

Thank you to the Genealogy Guys, George Morgan and Drew Smith. Your podcasts have informed and inspired me. I appreciate that you have taken the time to encourage my speaking and book writing efforts.

Thanks to Linda J. for editorial and research support. I consider cousins of my cousins to be my cousins, too.

My appreciation goes to Colonel John and the Reverend Lili Bush, for the friendship from your whole family to a young flight test engineer way back when. Thanks, John, for letting me borrow your interesting ancestors to illustrate Google searches in my lectures and in this book.

Thanks, as always, to my one-stop shopping for technical assistance, editorial skills and moral support, Sharon Gumerove. Your rates are too reasonable. Your encouragement is priceless.

INTRODUCTION

Genealogy was always a part of our family life. We heard stories about my Mother's Mother and Father and the colorful people in the family. There were tales of my legendary great-great-grandfather, an immigrant from Ireland who was trained as a mathematician, worked as a coachman, and ran a night school in Newport, Rhode Island. Listening to their stories motivated me to learn more about them. The lack of similar tales from my Father's side of the family was also motivating.

Living through the life events that generate vital records, I grew to better understand how births, marriages, and deaths change a family and redefine the relationships of its members. Children grow up to be parents; children may become care givers to their former care givers; and there are people we have known who will never know each other because they occupied the planet at different times. These events pushed me into the study of genealogy, to become a bridge for those in my life who were born without knowing their grandparents or other ancestors.

At the time of my marriage, I purchased a well-known family tree program that came with several CDs. One of those CDs contained a family tree that had my father in it. Recently, I had the chance to personally thank that second cousin, once removed, for submitting our family tree. We enjoyed a cousins' reunion which was made possible by the contributions of all the cousins who had collaborated to find each other.

Then the Ellis Island records came online. They fed my burgeoning interest as I located immigration records about my ancestors. The importance of the family unit was illustrated by the migration patterns I saw.

When my son was born I wanted to be able to tell him the stories of our family. That required evaluating what I had heard, determining what was true and what was fiction. This required evidence. The next step was building on the truth to flesh out the details of their lives.

This book is intended to assist your efforts to become the bridge between generations past and to come. You can inspire those to come by sharing the triumphs and challenges of previous generations, and making the history in books come to life with your ancestors, rather than unknown characters who appear on a piece of paper.

As with my other book, *A Week of Genealogy: Things to Know and Do Online and Offline*, the activities can be done over a series of weekends, or even on weekdays. Some efforts may prove very fruitful; for example, you may choose to devote several days to censuses. In fact, you will probably revisit censuses and Internet searching over and over again during your genealogical research. Both of these activities focus on using the Internet, although some census research can be done in a combination of online and offline efforts.

This book contains activities for your weekend of genealogy, including Friday Night, Saturday and Sunday. There are also activities for going beyond the main activities on Saturday and Sunday.

Prior to Saturday and Sunday, I recommend that you do the Friday Night activities before you start hunting for censuses or searching the Internet, so that you have the information you have already gathered at your fingertips. When you find a record, you will be able to cross check it against the information you already know, and verify that it is for your ancestor.

Saturday's principal activity focuses on United States Federal Censuses. A census record is a snapshot of life as the family knew it. Federal Census records are popular because of the data they include, and because they are taken every ten years. They have always been very special to me. I was the only engineer in a family of liberal arts majors. One afternoon, I found a census record for my great-grandfather. He had immigrated to the US from Germany and listed his occupation as ... Engineer. When I discovered that I was not the only engineer in our family, it provided a meaningful link to a member of the family I had never met.

Sunday's primary activity is to use Internet search engines to scour the Web for content outside of the subscription services. For this day, you will find details about searching the Internet using Google, Mocavo, and other search engines. Websites and other content can be added to the Internet at any time, so these searches should be done every few months. You will learn ways to automate the searches, and to resurrect pages that no longer exist.

Websites can change their appearance at any time. This is especially true of two of the significant websites discussed in this book, Ancestry.com and Google. I encourage you to focus on the main concepts presented in this book, as those will stay the same. While I have given my best effort to keep this book as up-to-date as possible, there are no guarantees that the web pages will be at the same addresses, or look the same as they do in this book. With that in mind, I have given search terms where appropriate.

Note: Search Terms
When a word is listed as a search term, type that word. When you see angular brackets around a word (< >), replace that word within the brackets with your own search term.

Search Terms:
 <state> "state census"
Use the word census and substitute the state where you are looking for state census records.
 Oregon "state census"
For a state with two words in its name, use quotes around the whole state name.
 "New York" "state census"

FRIDAY NIGHT:
Get Ready

Tonight, get ready for the weekend by reviewing the information you have and putting it into a quick reference format for Saturday and Sunday. A pedigree chart and timelines will be valuable to help you as you search for your ancestors in the census records, or construct searches on the Internet.

Pedigree Chart

This type of chart contains your direct lineage and it is often used as a starting place for research. A pedigree chart begins with you. Next, you add your mother and father, and then add each parent's mother and father. Over the weekend, you may be adding more direct ancestors to this chart. You can find examples of blank pedigree charts on several websites.

Search terms: pedigree chart

When the people on the pedigree chart are numbered, it is called an Ahnentafel Chart (Figure 1). Ahnentafel is German for "ancestor table". You start by numbering yourself 1. Your father is 2, and your mother is 3. Your father's father is 4, and his mother is 5. Your mother's father is 6, her mother is 7. Notice that you always list the father first numerically. After you, all the males on the chart (fathers) will have even numbers, and all the females on the chart (mothers) will have odd numbers.

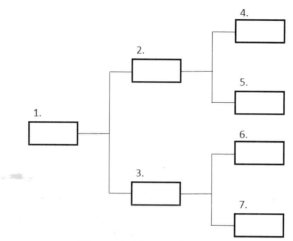

Figure 1. Ahnentafel Chart.

Pedigree charts typically include 4, 5 or 6 generations. The last on the right side of the page, is used as the first person, or root, on a new pedigree chart. Each pedigree chart has a place for you to enter a number identifying the page number of that chart, and what number the first person has on a preceding chart. These numbers guide you in fitting the multiple charts together.

Under each box on the pedigree chart you can enter birth, marriage and death dates and places, as shown in Figure 2.

Figure 2. Pedigree/Ahnentafel birth, marriage, death information.

This numbering scheme can also be helpful in organizing notebooks for the papers that you collect. Number the dividers in the notebook using the Ahnentafel numbers, and store paper relating to the ancestor to allow quick retrieval.

Pedigree charts are also helpful in visualizing how DNA is inherited. The Y-chromosome is passed along the line from father-to-son, which can be found by tracing the top line of boxes in a pedigree chart. The mitochondrial DNA is passed from mother-to-daughter, which can be seen in the line of boxes at the bottom of a pedigree chart.

Timelines
Timelines allow you to focus on one ancestor. A timeline shows the dates and locations of his or her life events. The best approach is to develop one for each ancestor, or at a minimum for the heads of households that you are researching. The next step is to draw a straight line, beginning with the ancestor's birth at one end, and death (and burial, if known) at the other end. Then, chronologically mark the dates of life events along the line, including the location of each event. Significant events can include birth, marriage, death, residences, immigration, education and military service. You can include whatever else you might find useful. For some ancestors there may be very little on the timeline when you begin.

A timeline containing biographical information for the poet Robert Frost is shown Figure 3. As census records are located, the timeline can be updated with residences and other data.

March 26, 1874	Born
1885	Moved with his mother and sister to eastern Massachusetts
1892	Attended Dartmouth College
1893 (?)	Went back home
December 1895	Married: Elinor Miriam White
1897	Entered Harvard
1901 (?)	Left Harvard
1906 to 1911	Worked at Pinkerton Academy
1911 to 1912	Lived in Plymouth, New Hampshire and taught at the New Hampshire Normal School
1912	Sailed with his family to Glasgow, and later settled in Beaconsfield
1916 to 1938	English professor at Amherst College
January 29, 1963	Died
	Buried: Old Bennington Cemetery

Figure 3. Timeline for Robert Frost.

A timeline also provides ideas about where and when to look for an ancestor. You can use an ancestor's timeline as a reference sheet (cheat sheet) to help you establish whether or not you have found the correct person, or an unrelated person with the same name.

Check the electronic family tree software program that you use; it may have a feature to generate timelines.

Keep Electronic Copies

I recommend keeping electronic copies of all data, whether downloaded from a website, received via an e-mail or acquired as a letter received in the mail and then scanned. I also recommend scanning your research notes. It is easier to store, post, duplicate, and share records in electronic format than on paper. Be sure to give your electronic files meaningful names.

Save A Web Page

Web Browsers have an option to save a page. For example, Internet Explorer has a File menu with a "Save as..." menu item.

Another way is to print the web page to a Portable Document Format (PDF) file. There are several free computer programs, such as pdf995. pdf995 prints the address of the web page, which is abbreviated if it is a very long address, and the date the page was accessed. Once pdf995 is installed, you select print in the browser, and then choose pdf995 in the printer dialog box. Another dialog box will open, enabling you to select a folder and a name for the file you are saving. With the free version of pdf995 you see ads during the conversion process; for a nominal fee you can get an ad-free version of the software. As of this writing it takes two steps to install the program on your computer. Always follow the installation directions on the website.

Search term: pdf995 download

SATURDAY:
The Federal Census

Saturday's activity is to find your ancestors in the Federal Census Population Schedules. Your goal on this day is to systematically gather the sets of available censuses for each ancestor. The details in this book are specific to the United States Federal Census, however several of the search strategies can also be used when investigating censuses from other countries. To get you prepared for the day of census activity, we will review why censuses were conducted, what you can find in the census records, and introduce the popular websites to find census records. The worksheet at the end of the chapter provides a format for you to use in a specific census search. The following chapters cover what to do if you cannot find your ancestor, and what to do with the data you obtain.

Purpose of the Census
Censuses have been taken throughout history, with the first known census taken in 3800 B.C. by the Babylonians. The Romans also took censuses; the Latin word *censere*, translates to estimate. The original reason for a government to take a census was to understand the population.

Censuses have been taken in the United States every 10 years, beginning in 1790. The Federal Census has been used to count the population; determine the demographics for legislative representation; decide how to disperse federal funds; and to calculate how many men would be available to serve in a war. In the twentieth century, a nineteenth-century census was used for planning for the social security system. A census can capture information about livestock and production, or gather public health data.

Over time, the Federal Census gathered more and more details about residents. These details can help us in our genealogical research by telling us about our ancestors' lives and giving us leads to find more of their records. The trend of detailed censuses was reversed in the 2010 Census, which had only ten questions and was probably the least useful to a genealogist.

Each census is released 72 years after it has been taken. This is in consideration of the privacy of the individuals included in it. The 1940 census was released in 2012, and the 1950 census will be released 10 years later, in 2022. In contrast, the censuses in the United Kingdom are not released for one hundred years.

This book focuses on population schedules. There have also been a variety non-population schedules: slave, industrial, manufacturing, agricultural, social and mortality. There were special schedules for military veterans of some wars and their widows. Some of these special schedules can be found online.

What's in the census?
The census contains information about your ancestors' family members, and their relationships. The census also provides depth about people and their lives: where they lived; who they lived near; what they did for an occupation; and of course, the family structure. From later censuses you can discover important life data about when they were born, married, immigrated and naturalized.

Do not neglect the information in the census about those ancestors who do not appear in your pedigree chart. These are your collateral ancestors. When you have trouble finding information about direct ancestors, the answers may be in the records of your uncles, aunts and cousins.

Censuses may solve puzzling problems. One of my favorite census finds is when a wife's parents are living with the family, potentially providing the wife's maiden name. But be cautious and keep an open mind, as a mother-in-law may have remarried.

Caveat: Pre-1850 Censuses

Before 1850 the only names on the census records are the heads of households. The rest of the family is hidden in tally marks made in gender and age columns. To make sure you have the correct family you have to look at these tally marks and review your information about the family.

For those pre-1850 censuses, an effective technique is to look forward, then look back. To accomplish this, locate the family in the 1850 census, and look at the ages of the parents and children. Subtract ten years from those ages and check against what you have in the 1840 Census; subtract twenty years and compare with what you have in the 1830 Census.

Caveat: The 1890 Census

The 1890 Federal Census was lost as a result of a fire at the storage location and the resulting water damage. Very little of the population schedule from that census still exists. The remaining fragments that have survived are for parts of: Alabama, the District of Columbia, Georgia, Illinois, Minnesota, New Jersey, New York, North Carolina, Ohio, South Dakota, and Texas. If your ancestor lived in an area of a state where fragments exist, remember to check the fragments.

The loss of the 1890 Federal Census is unfortunate. At that point in time, there was a lot of movement in my family, as this was the case in many other families. That census would be a great resource to have.

Remember, we are looking for the information that is contained in a record, so do not give up just because one type of record does not exist. In many cases you can reconstruct elements of the census data from city directories and other substitutes. With that in mind, Ancestry.com has compiled an 1890 Census Substitute. The landing page allows you to search a group of city directories, state censuses, voting lists and other records from one page, http://search.ancestry.com/search/group/1890census

Bonus: The 1940 5% Sampling and Double Census

The 1940 Federal Census is special for a few reasons. It was the most recently released census, so it is the shortest bridge back in time to the current day. Five percent of the population, which was two people on each page, were selected to answer supplemental questions that included information about their parents, native language, veteran status, social security, and occupation. Women also answered detailed questions relating to their marriage(s) and children. You may be the person who wins the genealogical lottery if your ancestor was chosen to answer these supplemental questions.

The 1940 Census is also a double census. To gather more information about how the Great Depression had influenced the movement of families, every person was asked for his or her residence on 1 April 1935.

A little background on accessing the records

Not too long ago, a genealogist would have to consult multiple indexes to determine which filmstrip held her ancestor's information. She would use the Soundex code, which we cover later in the book, for the ancestor's surname, and then consult a filmstrip with an index showing which filmstrips contain that surname. Loading each of those filmstrips in question, she would have to scroll through images to find the actual page with the entries she sought. The filmstrip identifier is still used as one way to identify census records. Since the Soundex code can be found in genealogical records, and is useful to help expand your avenues of search, this book will devote a little time in a later section to demonstrate it to you.

Using digitized records, searching for ancestors in the census is now much easier. The key to finding records more easily is the indexing of each person, or each head of household, in the census. Having the digitized records online is another leap; we now can search for and view records from home at any time of the day or night.

When we search for a person in the census, we are searching in an index for the census. Depending on the website we use, this index entry may have a link to the record itself. Creating indexes to the records, known as indexing, has been done by the content providers who have paid companies to do it, or by crowdsourcing done by volunteers. The process of indexing can introduce errors from omission to human mistakes in misinterpreting handwriting.

Where to find Federal Census Records and Indexes

The Federal Census records from 1790 to 1940 were microfilmed by the National Archives and Records Administration (NARA) and are available for viewing. From my perspective, the most convenient place to view them is online.

There are several websites that contain census records. Example websites are: Ancestry.com, Fold3 (now owned by Ancestry.com), HeritageQuest, FamilySearch, Archives.com, and MyHeritage. While the online offerings are the easiest ways to find records, they can still be accessed by the filmstrips. If you have no way to access the records themselves online, you can use FamilySearch to locate the index entry, and hunt down the records themselves on filmstrips or at a subscription service available at a library or a Family History Center. You can find the location of a Family History Center at https://familysearch.org/locations/centerlocator.

This book will cover how to access census records through the indexes of Ancestry.com, HeritageQuest, and FamilySearch. Other websites where you might find transcriptions of the records are also covered. Finding a transcription is a good lead, but you will want to get a copy of the actual census record.

Check your local public library for subscriptions to Ancestry.com and HeritageQuest. The Library edition of Ancestry.com may be available for you to use for free at the local branch of your library. Your library may also subscribe to HeritageQuest which is usually accessible at the library or from home through the library's web site. Another place to check for subscriptions to these databases is at a local Family History Center.

The Ancestry.com subscription website has images for all of the United States Federal Censuses from 1790 to 1940, and every name is indexed. Signing up for a free account allows you to search and view the list of results. With a free account you can also view the images only for the 1880 and 1940 Federal Censuses. A free account has another benefit: you will be notified if any of the paid databases is available for free. Free access is usually scheduled over a national holiday weekend.

FamilySearch offers online indexes for all censuses. FamilySearch has images for the 1870, 1900, and 1940 Federal Censuses. From a Family History Center you can access images of the other censuses.

Mocavo, the genealogical search engine, has indexes for all censuses.

Methodology

As in other genealogical research, the methodology is to start at the most recent event, and work backward. A timeline will be useful as you look for the ancestor or family unit in the most recent census available, and trace that unit back as far back in time as you can go. When an ancestor is living with parents, your pedigree chart will also help to verify that you have located the correct ancestor.

Get your timeline, or at least a list of the people in the family. Having birth, marriage and death dates on your list will help. Knowing the family structure can help you be sure that the records you have found are for the correct individuals.

Pick the most recent released census in which they would appear. For most of us, that is the 1940 Federal Census. Begin searching using one of the products below. If all you find is an index entry, remember to make a plan to obtain the original record.

Work your way back in time through the censuses. Trace for one line of a family at a time, just to keep your sanity. Do not forget that the collateral relatives' census records can provide useful information.

Try your search using basic names and locations. If an ancestor is elusive, the next chapter offers strategies to find him or her.

Federal Censuses on Ancestry.com

Depending on how you think and how you search, there are multiple ways to find your ancestor in the Federal Census on Ancestry.com.

The first option is to enter information on the home page. The second option is to limit your search to census and voters lists. The third option is to use the advanced search option and add specific information about your ancestors to narrow in on limited results.

I usually do not recommend the latter approach. I prefer to start big, with broad search terms, and refine the search after I review the results. Be cautious when you use the Advanced Search; you might miss interesting results. By specifying a value for one of the fields that is not contained in a record type, none of the records of that type will be returned in the results. By specifying a value for a field be matched exactly, the results will not contain records that might have a different value due to being incorrectly transcribed, or having information that does not match what you expected. However, using the Advanced Search for an ancestor with a common name can be an effective strategy you can use.

Ancestry.com recommends that searches start small and expand by using their search filters. They recommend using the exact match settings to restrict results to having the name spelled exactly as it appears in the search, and the limiting the year(s) of the record. If you do not find what you are looking for, you can increase the number of results by including sound-alike names, or increasing the date range, or variations on the location.

The different search approaches are described in more detail in the next section. Your repeated use of Ancestry.com will undoubtedly enable you to develop your own search style.

However you find a record, I recommend saving the electronic version for future use. If you have made an online family tree at the website you located the record, you can attached the census to it.

Searching Ancestry.com

One way is to start on the home page and search for all the records, then narrow down using the filters on the left side of the browser (Figure 4). These filters allow you to limit results by the categories they come from and the years of the records.

The second way to start is to click and hold the Search button near the top of any page and it will display a dropdown menu of categories of records, shown in Figure 5. From the menu select "Census & Voter Lists" to go to the Search page for census and voter list records.

Another way to search for records is from the Search page. From the home page, left click on the Search button. On the search page, scroll down to see the section labeled Explore by Location. When the USA tab above the map is selected, you will see a map of the US and a list of the states (Figure 6). By clicking on a state on the map, or on a link, you can see the databases Ancestry.com has for that state, and select one to search.

Figure 4. Filters for Ancestry.com Search Results.

Figure 5. Ancestry.com Search Drop-Down Box.

There are also tabs above the map for: UK & Ireland; Europe; Canada; and Australia & NZ. These tabs are allow you to explore the databases for those specific locations.

Figure 6. Ancestry.com Explore by Location.

If you want to add more information about your ancestors to narrow in on the specific record, an advanced search can be done from the Search page.

However you choose to begin your search, the results page will present a list of results. Each result contains a link to a page that contains a transcription of the record, and a link to the record itself. When you let your mouse hover the mouse over a result, you can look at a preview for the record. The preview can help you determine whether you want to click through to see the record, which can save you the download time for an irrelevant record when you are on the shared at a library or have a slow Internet connection.

For this weekend day's activity, use the drop-down menu from the Search button and select "Census & Voter Lists". The Census & Voter Lists Search Page is shown in Figure 7. Since your focus is census records, this is a good place to start.

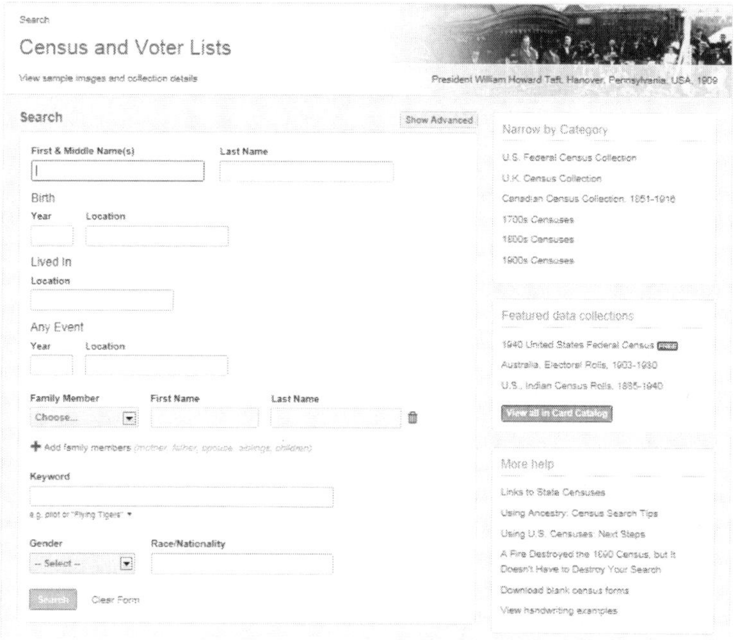

Figure 7. Ancestry.com Census & Voter Lists Search Page.

Ancestry.com Filters

Ancestry.com's Search Sliders determine how the information entered the search box fields is used by search filters (Figure 8). The information in the fields can be used as part of a broad search, where results contain your search terms and ones similar to them, or in an exact search, where only the records with those exact words are returned. You can place your mouse on the slider, and move it slowly along the line from side to side to see the points and their labels. Remember to click Update when you change a setting. Selecting a category of records in list below the filters will reset the Filters, which can be seen in the position of the sliders.

There are filter for name, year, and place. For the name field the options are: Not Exact; Exact, similar, sounds like, and initials; Exact, sounds like, and similar; Exact and similar; and Exact. For the year field the options are: Not exact; +/- 10 years; +/- 5 years; +/- 2 years; +/- 1 years; and Exact. For the place field the inputs

Figure 8. Ancestry.com Search Filters.

are: Not exact, Country; State; State and adjacent states; County and adjacent counties; and County.

Mocavo also provides the use of similar sliders to filter search results.

There is also a dropdown menu for collections, where you can choose a country, or ethnicity (Figure 9). You can select United States for these searches, to limit the results to the US Collections.

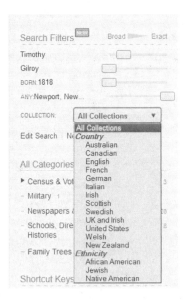

Figure 9. Ancestry.com Filter by Collection.

Wildcards

You can specify patterns of letters to use in your searches with wildcards. An * specifies that 0 or more characters can appear in that position in your results. A ? is a single-character wildcard that specifies that the results have any one letter in that position.

When I want to search for results with variations of McMahon like McMahan and McMan, I use the search term: McMa*

To look for variations of McMahon with the same number of letters, varying in only position, such as McMahon or McMahan, my search string is McMah?n

Whenever you use wildcards, be sure to check the specific database's rules for using them.

Ancesty.com allows you to use the wildcard character (*) at the beginning of a name, or the end of the name, but not both. There must be three characters that are not wildcards in the name. The * will return from 0 to 5 characters in that position in the name. Wildcards will not work when you specify Soundex searches.

FamilySearch allows up to three * in the name, but like Ancestry.com, the name must contain three characters that are not wildcards in the name. A wildcard can appear as the first character of the name.

Note: If your ancestor's family appears at the bottom of a census record, remember to check the next page in case there are additional members of the family. In-laws, servants and others are usually listed after the youngest child of the head of household. Similarly, if your ancestor appears at the top of a census page, look at the previous page for other family members.

Example: Ancestry.com search for Robert Frost

In this example I searched for census records for one of my Father's favorite poets, Robert Frost. When I started research into this New England poet's life, I was surprised to learn that he was born in San Francisco, California and moved to New England as an adult. However, I learned from the census that his father was born in New England.

I built a timeline for Robert Frost, shown in Figure 10, using the biographic information about him I had collected. You would do this from the data you have collected about your ancestor's life. I extracted dates and locations for the events in his life, as well as his residences, employment and education. This timeline can help when you find people having the same name in a records. You may have to determine if it is the same person, or a person who happened to have the same name. A timeline may also provide ideas for locations to look for an ancestor when he or she does not appear with the expected family unit.

March 26, 1874	Born
1885	Moved with his mother and sister to eastern Massachusetts
1892	Attended Dartmouth College
1893 (?)	Went back home
December 1895	Married: Elinor Miriam White
1897	Entered Harvard
1901 (?)	Left Harvard
1906 to 1911	Worked at Pinkerton Academy
1911 to 1912	Lived in Plymouth, New Hampshire and taught at the New Hampshire Normal School
1912	Sailed with his family to Glasgow, and later settled in Beaconsfield
1916 to 1938	English professor at Amherst College
January 29, 1963	Died
	Buried: Old Bennington Cemetery

Figure 10. Timeline for Robert Frost.

On the Census & Voter Lists search page I entered his name and birth year of 1874, and click search. On the upper left of the results page, I notice that that the sliders are set to "Broad" for his first name and born date, and "Exact, sounds like and similar" for his last name. Ancestry.com allows you to narrow down the search to be in censuses for a specific century or a decade. I know that the first census that he should appear in was 1880, and he should be about 6 years old, so I selected 1880. By hovering the mouse over a result to look at the preview, I checked if the data matched what I knew about the individual. Then I clicked to view the partial transcription of the original record (Figure 11). From there, I clicked the option to view the original records (Figure 12).

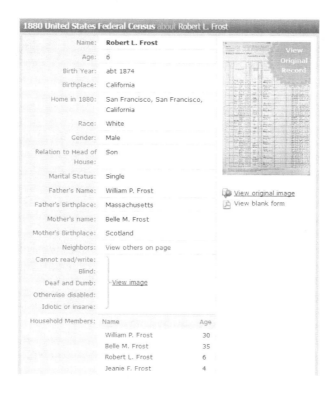

Figure 11. Ancestry.com 1880 Federal Census Robert Frost Trancription.

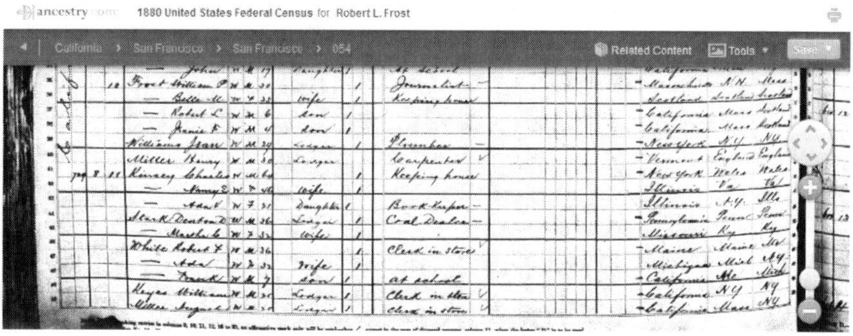

Figure 12. Ancestry.com 1880 Federal Census for Robert Frost.

Ancestry.com displays a breadcrumb trail above the record, which shows you the city, the county, the state, and the year of the census. This allows you a way to navigate through the images from different enumeration districts, or different counties.

When you save the image of the record, use a meaningful file name. The words in your filename are potentially searchable, so it is well worth using descriptive and long filenames. The names need to be meaningful to you. Example words and phrases to include are: the year of the census, the fact that it is a Federal Census for the United States, and the names of the people involved. You can also include the place where they resided in your filename. For example:

1930 US Census Arthur + Margaret Gilroy Brooklyn.jpg

When you find a record, you can save it, share it, print it, or attach it to an Ancestry.com online family tree. By clicking on Save, you have the option to save it your computer, or attach a record that you find to a person on an online tree that you have built on their website. The details of a census record can be difficult to read when you print it out on an 8½ x 11-inch sheet of paper; you can enlarge the image many times over when you have it stored on your own computer.

You can share a record via social media or e-mail. When you share a record by selecting the envelope above the Save button, a link is sent via e-mail to the address you specify. The recipient using the link does not have to be a subscriber to view the record. There is a limit on how many records an address can receive per month. This can be a handy feature if you forget to bring a USB drive to the library; you can e-mail the links to the records to yourself.

When you attach a record to your tree, those people who have been invited to your tree can view those attached records even if they are not subscribers.

Ancestry.com Card Catalog

Another way to search on Ancestry.com for results in a specific census, or in a specific database, is to use the Card Catalog. The Card Catalog allows you to select a database, and to confine your search to that one database.

Click on the Search option and select Card Catalog from the dropdown menu. In the Keyword(s) field enter the year and census (e.g. 1880 Census). A list of databases that have those keywords in their title is displayed. The results list can be sorted by using the Sort By dropdown menu. By default the list is shown sorted by popularity, however you can also view the results by: Database Title; Date Updated; Date Added; or Record Count. Click on the name of the database you want to search, and enter your ancestor's data in the search page.

Using the Card Catalog to search an individual database can be a useful technique. You can use the card catalog to find out about other relevant databases on Ancestry.com's website, like state censuses. One of the key features of the search page for any database is the description of the database. The description may save you time and frustration if the database does not cover the year of an event in an ancestor's life, or the geographic area where your ancestor lived.

Free Databases on Ancestry.com
There are over 700 free databases on Ancestry.com. Both the indexes and the images are free for these databases. Some of the databases are free because they have been indexed by the World Archives Project community, or are JewishGen and Rootsweb.org databases that are hosted on Ancestry.com servers. The War of 1812 Pension applications on Fold3.com are also free. You can search all the free databases from a landing page, or you can choose an individual database from the list. You will need a free account to search and access these databases. The web page is: search.ancestry.com/search/group/FreeIndexAcom.

HeritageQuest
HeritageQuest is another subscription service, with genealogical databases: the Census, Books, the Periodical Source Index (PERSI), Freeman's Bank records, Revolutionary War records, and the US Serial Set (Figure 13). ProQuest sells subscriptions to HeritageQuest only to institutions, such as library systems. If your library does subscribe, you should be able to access HeritageQuest from home, by using your library card. In contrast, Ancestry.com is selling individual subscriptions, so the Ancestry.com Library version can be accessed only while you are physically present at the subscribing library.

Ask your librarian, or check your local library's website to look for which electronic databases subscriptions they have. With the growing interest in genealogy, your local library might subscribe to a set of content providers that are related to genealogy.

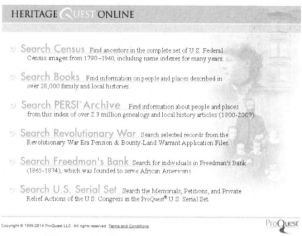

Figure 13. Heritage Quest Databases.

Keep in mind that many of the censuses at HeritageQuest have an index that lists only the heads of each household. That means you may not be able to search for the person in the family who has an unusual name.

Go to the HeritageQuest homepage and choose the search census link. From the Search Census page there are three types of searches you can perform: basic search, advanced search, or find it by page number. The basic search has fields to search on the surname, given name, census year and state (Figure 14). The advanced search has fields for additional details about the ancestor such an age, race, sex, and birthplace. I caution you to use this with care, because you do not want to exclude too many search results. There is also an option to view censuses for those who have previously used microfilms of censuses, and know the filmstrip series, roll number, and page number of the census record.

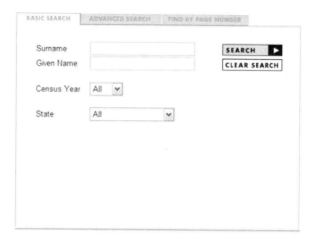

Figure 14. HeritageQuest Basic Census Search.

Select Browse under the Census Tab to peruse the Census. Follow the steps to sequentially select from the drop-down menu: the year, the state, the county and the location (Figure 15). You can view Census records this way, which may be helpful if you are having a difficult time finding people who live in a small location. Due to the number of images for Manhattan, New York, this might not be a useful approach when trying to locate an ancestor who might have lived there. In a small village, where few people owned large tracts of land, this can be an effective approach.

Different databases have different front ends, which mean that each database may have the fields for entering information in a different order. In other words, take a look and be sure that you are entering the last name in the surname field and not in the first name field. Of course, switching the names intentionally can be a good search technique in case the indexer made that mistake when indexing the names.

Figure 15. HeritageQuest Browse Census.

Example: HeritageQuest Search

I did a basic search for my ancestor John Small in the 1900 Federal Census. I entered the following:

Surname: Small
Given Name: John
Census Year: 1900
State: New York

HeritageQuest presented me with a list of the counties in New York State where the name John Small appeared in their index of the 1900 Federal Census. From his timeline, I knew he lived in Brooklyn, which is also known as Kings County. I selected Kings County, and saw that there were two men of that name in the county. Since I knew his approximate birth year, the older gentleman better fit his age at that time. I clicked on the appropriate link to see the record.

HeritageQuest may have a statement above the image to alert you that: "The name you've found is on 1 of 2 subpages." There are tabs for Subpage A and Subpage B, so be patient and check both of them for your ancestor.

There are a pair of buttons labeled Positive or Negative to change between viewing the image as black text on a white background, or as white text on a black background. This option is useful when you are having a problem deciphering the handwriting. Viewing white-on-black instead of black-on-white can make the handwriting easier to read. There are also print and download options. You can download the records in two formats, TIFF File and PDF File.

Ancestry.com vs. HeritageQuest

There are certainly other databases containing the Federal Census records, such as Fold3.com, Findmypast.com, and HeritageQuest.com. This book compares only the two databases offered for free by many public libraries. Ancestry.com has the advantage of an every name index, but you must use it while you are at the subscribing library. HeritageQuest can usually be accessed from home with a library card number issued by a subscribing library. HeritageQuest has only a head-of-household index for most of the censuses, and part of the 1930 Federal Census is missing. If your library has both, I recommend that you use Ancestry.com when you are at the library, and when you are at home see how far you can get with HeritageQuest.

Some Family History Centers have access to subscription databases; contact your local one to see what products are available.

FamilySearch

FamilySearch has a landing page for U.S. Federal Census research at https://familysearch.org/census/us (Figure 16), where you can search indexes. However, you can only view the actual Federal Census records for 1850, 1890, and 1930. Censuses from other years, can be viewed on other subscription websites, or in one of the many Family History Centers.

Figure 16. FamilySearch U.S. Federal Census Landing Page.

On the landing page, look for the section labeled Find Your Ancestors in the Following Collections, then click on the year to view a link to search the index for that census.

After you enter terms on the search page, you will see a list of results. For every result there will be a partial transcription.

Although a statement next to the link for searching a census index may state: Image Access Available, the images may not be available to you from the FamilySearch website. If you select to browse through the images for the censuses not available from FamilySearch, you will see digital folders, but when you try to open them you will get a message that the image is viewable at Ancestry.com or when using the website while you are at a Family History Center.

There are additional supplemental census information for 1850, 1890, and 1930 (Figure 17). I was able to access images for the 1850 Mortality Schedules on the website. Remember that only fragments of the 1890 Federal Census have survived.

Find Your Ancestors in the Following Collections

1790 1800 1810 1820 1830 1840 **1850** 1860 1870 1880 1890 1900 1910 1920 1930 1940

★ United States Census (Mortality Schedule), 1850 *Image Access Available*
★ United States Census (Slave Schedule), 1850 *Image Access Available*
★ United States Census, 1850 *Image Access Available*

Find Your Ancestors in the Following Collections

1790 1800 1810 1820 1830 1840 1850 1860 1870 1880 **1890** 1900 1910 1920 1930 1940

★ United States, 1890 Census of Union Veterans and Widows of the Civil War *Image Access Available*
★ United States Census, 1890 *Image Access Available*

Find Your Ancestors in the Following Collections

1790 1800 1810 1820 1830 1840 1850 1860 1870 1880 1890 1900 1910 1920 **1930** 1940

★ United States Census of Merchant Seamen, 1930 *Image Access Available*
★ United States Census, 1930 *Image Access Available*

Figure 17. FamilySearch links for 1850, 1890, and 1930 U.S. Census.

Search for Your Ancestors

Now that you have reviewed what you are searching for, and how to use the Ancestry.com, HeritageQuest and FamilySearch, give it a try. If you want to have a crib sheet to keep your focus on a family or individual, in a specific census, you can use the worksheet on the next page.

Specific Census Worksheet

When you are searching in one census, you will want keep your focus limited to the set of family members alive and living together at the time, and their location, if known. You may not have all the information when you start searching censuses, and may add details as you go back in time. You may choose to organize the data you know in this cheat sheet.

Year of the census

_____

Ancestor's name

_____

Ancestor's birthdate and birthplace (state or country)

_____

Family members that are living with the ancestor (if known)

_____

_____

_____

Expected location (state, county, city, address)

_____

Alternate location (if applicable)

_____

Surname variations using wildcards

_____

SATURDAY:
Where is Your Ancestor?

Some ancestors are easier to find than others. When you have used the basic techniques from the previous chapter and an ancestor still eludes you, do not give up. In this chapter, we will review all the ways that errors may be introduced as the information flows from the ancestor to you. The process begins with the reliability of the people who gave the information, those who recorded and copied it to official forms, and those who transcribed it for indexes. By anticipating and compensating for these errors, we increase the probability locating our ancestors.

Errors

The person providing information to the enumerator is the first way an error on the record may occur. Perhaps the five-year-old in the family spoke to the enumerator, or maybe it was a neighbor who gave the information because your ancestors were out and about. Assessing the quality of the informant became easier in the 1940 Federal Census, because there is a circled x next to the family member who provided data to the enumerator.

The next source of error is the person recording it. The enumerator might have written down a name phonetically, which led to a spelling error.

Later, the enumerator would take the notes made during the visit and copy the data on to the sheets he or she was going to submit. Sometimes an enumerator might have been required to submit multiple copies of the census. Copying the names and other data from notes to the sheets they were submitting was another opportunity for error.

Then there are errors related to using online records. These online records are valuable because of the indexing of all the names in the records. However, when an indexer is looking at an original record, the handwriting on it can be difficult to decipher. A mistake in the first letter can create a major obstacle to finding a surname, so keep in mind trying wildcards when you search.

The Old Days of Census Research

For perspective, it is worth revisiting how census records were accessed prior to them being available on the Internet. First, the researcher would calculate the Soundex code for the last name of her ancestor. Then she would go to the Soundex microfilm for that census. She would locate the roll for that state with the Soundex code on it. Then she would scroll to the entry for the ancestor and locate a card that had been indexed for the ancestor. From that card, she would copy the volume number, the enumeration district, the sheet number and the line number. Finally she would go to the actual rolls of census data, and scroll to that sheet number and then find the entry.

Today, a researcher can enter the web address for a database, enter search data on a webpage, select the result with the ancestor's name, and access an electronic image of the census with a mouse click. I think you will agree this is a much, much easier way to access census records.

Soundex Code

The Soundex algorithm uses one letter and three numbers to represent a surname. The code uses the first letter of a surname, and then uses numbers in place of the next three consonant sounds in a name to represent how the surname sounds. Soundex codes were important in accessing census records, and can still be used to visualize how names can be misspelled.

Mapping all the surnames in the 1880 Federal Census to a Soundex code started as part of a Works Project Administration (WPA) Project. The code was used in the 1930's by Congress before Social Security legislation was enacted to calculate how many people might qualify for benefits. Researchers were sent to the 1880 census to look for families with children aged ten and below. The children of that age would be the people who would soon be eligible for Social Security benefits. The Soundex code was a handy way to index names, and it was a used in subsequent censuses as well.

To calculate the Soundex code, write out your surname. Keep the first letter; that is the first character in the Soundex code. Then cross out any remaining vowels (a, e, i, o, u) in your surname, and cross out the y's. Also, cross out the letters that are h or w. There is a variation of the h and w rule, where if one comes between two letters that are mapped to the same Soundex code, you cross out that second letter, as it is usually not pronounced. In cases where the h and w are not used this way, the second consonant can be encoded. The numbers substituted for the letters that remain are shown in Table 1. Ignore any letters after the first four consonants. If you have less than 3 numbers, place 0's on the end of your result until you have three numbers after the first letter.

Table 1. Soundex Code for Consonants.

Replace these letters	with the number
B, P, F, V	1
C, S, K, G, J, Q, X, Z	2
D, T	3
L	4
M, N	5
R	6

Example: Calculating the Soundex Code for McMahon

I crossed out the vowels, and any y's, h's and w's that are in McMahon.

M C M X̶ H̶ O̶ N

The first letter is M, so that is the first character in the Soundex code for the surname. Then I mapped the remaining letters to numbers. C becomes a 2, M becomes a 5, and N becomes a 5. The Soundex code for McMahon is M255.

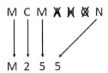

Example: Calculating the Soundex Code for Jones

I crossed out the vowels, and any y's, h's and w's that are in Jones. I kept the first letter, and mapped the remaining consonants to numbers.

Since there are fewer than three consonants to map to numbers, I added a zero is added to the end. The Soundex code for Jones is M220.

You Try It

Generate the Soundex code for your last name. There are a couple of ways to check your calculation. Some states use the Soundex code as part of each driver's license number. There are also Soundex calculators available online.

Search terms: Soundex calculator

Although the Soundex code is no longer needed to search for a census entry, there is a reason you might choose to understand the code. By mapping the numbers in the Soundex code back to letters, you might be able to visualize alternate spellings of your name that you might not have thought to use.

Generating misspellings of a surname may help you find your ancestors. The Soundex for McMahon code is M255. Reversing it maps to the letters M C M N. Those letters suggest variations in spelling the surname: McMan, McMann, McMahan. As the Soundex code suggests, all these spelling variations sounds alike. Any vowels in combination, or double letters will sound alike.

The Daitch-Mokotoff Soundex (D-M Soundex) is an algorithm for encoding Germanic or Slavic surnames, which can be helpful for Jewish or Eastern European names.

Surnames with Prefixes

When you cannot locate someone who has a surname that includes a prefix such as Mc, O', Van or VanDer, try omitting the prefix when you search. For example, if your search for an O'Reilly is unsuccessful, try searching for Reilly. Another technique I have used for Mc or Mac prefixes is to insert a blank space after the prefix, so rather than McMahon I searched for Mc Mahon.

Finding Women in the Census

Always review what you know about a person to locate her or him in the census. For women, knowing when they married leads you to stop looking for them in their parents' home and start looking for them with a husband. Use their married, not their maiden names. Remember to search for unusual first names and birth places, or unusual names for children or siblings. Keep in mind that a woman's maiden name may be the name of an older couple that is living with her family in later life.

When viewing a woman and the youngest members of a family unit with the same surname, keep in mind women's childbearing ages. If the range of children's ages is very long, the husband may have remarried and started a second family. The youngsters might be grandchildren. If the young children living with a family are a married daughter's children, you may learn the son-in-law's surname.

They Are Still Missing
In addition to problems related to an enumerator or an indexer misinterpreting names, a person may have been omitted from a census.

If a family group is completely missing, you may be searching for them in the wrong location. That is where timelines can be helpful. If a census falls between the approximate time that a family changed their residence, and you know where they started and ended their relocation, you can search in both locations. Remember to search in intermediate places between those locations.

If a family cannot be located in the same place you expected them, and you believe that they did not move, there are a few tricks to try. If the database has flexibility in which fields can be filled in, try searching for a family member's first name in a locality. If the number of names in the results becomes cumbersome, try looking for one of the children who has an unusual name. Also try a search using just the first name of a parent and his or her birthplace in a geographic location.

Renowned genealogist Elizabeth Shown Mills recommends researching a person's FAN club: the friends, associates and neighbors. So, another strategy is to search for the neighbors, as there may be some link between the families, or they may still be living in proximity to each other. Search for the neighbors in a census immediately preceding or following the one where you cannot find the family. Then search for those neighbors in the census where you cannot find your family of interest. It may that neither family has moved, and you will find your ancestors in an adjacent house, having been omitted by an indexer. Or, the families may be associated, and moved together. An advantage of investigating the neighbors is finding a family that intermarried with yours; people tended to marry those who were geographically close to them.

Birthplace
Mistakes in birthplaces can be misleading, and cause you to discard the census result when it really is for your ancestor. People had to give the name of their birthplace as it was known at the time of the census, not what it was called when they were born. For

example, a person who was born in Germany may be listed as being born in Poland, Russia, or Germany, depending on the changing border. Another change you might see is a person listed as a Subject of Great Britain changing to being from an Irish Free State.

Examples: Search for a Different Family Member

I had a problem with finding my Great-Grandfather in the 1900 Federal Census. From my Grandfather's birth certificate, he and his family lived in Manhattan in 1898. I also knew that the family did move to Brooklyn, NY, before the 1910 census. I was convinced that they were still living in Manhattan, so I looked for his wife, my Great-Grandmother, Mary A Gilroy. I found her in the census, and discovered that instead of being listed as John George Gilroy, my Great-Grandfather was listed as George Gilroy. This search strategy is only successful if every name in the census is indexed; a wife would not appear in an index where only the heads of households are indexed.

In one census, my Grandmother was not shown with her family. I devised many theories about where she might have been, but the simple explanation was that the columns in the census had been transposed. In the census one of her twin brothers was 10 and the other 17, which was a clue that the columns had been shifted when they were copied by the enumerator.

Too Many Results

If you get too many results, limit your searches by using the search filters, or adding more data. You might start your searches with a surname and a state. Then you can limit your results by geographic locations, or use a first name or first initial instead of just a surname. Remember to try searching for a first name and a birthplace.

If you have too few results, start by taking out those limiting conditions. Take out the birthplace, take out the first name, and consider using wildcards in the surname.

One More Thing to Try

Type the first name in the last name field, and vice versa. If the indexer did the same thing, you will find your ancestor.

The Last Resort

There is one last resort: search the whole enumeration district (ED). I have done this a couple of times and it works better when the ancestor lives in a small village rather than in New York City. Locate the ED for the place where you believe your ancestor lived. One place to find an ED is Steve Morse's One-Step webpages at http://stevemorse.org. Use the address you think they lived at to find the enumeration district. Go to Image 1 of that ED and search the enumeration district, page by page.

Corrupted Data

There are other errors that can occur online. The image may be linked improperly, so that when you click on a search result, a different image appears on your screen. Another issue is that the image itself may be corrupted and not able to be viewed. If either of those errors occurs, notify the database owners. There may be a link on the web page itself to report a problem.

Last Thoughts

Some families were in motion. Keep in mind that the census was a snapshot of the country in one day. It is possible that your ancestors were counted twice or not at all. In her book, *The Guide to the Federal Census*, Kathleen Hinckley states that 10% of the urban population and 5% of the rural population that were missed completely. There are other estimates that as much as 15% of the population may not have been enumerated.

Remember your search terms. Keep track of them, and write them down or save them in a word processing document. If you ever have to find the ancestors again, you can retrace your steps. If your searches were unsuccessful, you do not have to waste time by using those unsuccessful search terms. Successful search terms can also be useful when looking for the ancestors in other databases.

BEYOND SATURDAY:
More to Do and More Censuses

The Federal Censuses provided a snapshot of a family or an individual every ten years. The snapshots included where and with whom they lived, where they were from, and what they were doing. When you have gathered these great records, and have enjoyed learning more about your ancestors, there is still more you can do with the censuses. You can organize the data you found, analyze it for connections, and leverage it to locate more information.

Family Trees
I recommend collecting all the data you uncover in a genealogy software program. If you have not yet started building an electronic version of your family tree, and want to, you have choices. You can find free genealogy software that you can download to build family trees on your computer, or find a website where you can build trees online. Either way, extract all the data out of the census records and enter it into your family tree.
Search term: genealogy software
When you transcribe any data, whether by typing it or by hand writing it, you have to look at it. When you look at data, you have a chance to think about what you see. This process may give you some new insights about your family. For example, look at the occupations and addresses of your ancestors. See if you can detect

a naming pattern that will help locate other branches or older generations of the family.

While I was entering the data for my Grandparents' families into the genealogy program on my computer, my Mother looked over my shoulder and pointed out that they lived on adjoining streets. She had not recalled how her parents had met; her parents knew each other from living in the same neighborhood.

When you are entering data from the census records into your electronic family tree, remember to cite your sources. You want to make sure that you actually know where to find these things again, and be able to prove to others that you found them. Be sure to cite exactly in which county, on which sheet, and on which line you found the information.

Deciphering the columns' headings of the scanned Federal Census records can be challenging. Ancestry.com, Family Tree Magazine, and other websites have blank Federal Census forms with clearer writing that are more easily readable. If you do not want to use an electronic family tree, you can also enter the data that you extract from a census onto a printed copy of the census form.

Finding More Data

In the Federal Census you can find approximate birth and marriage dates. For example, the 1900 Federal Census contains the month and year of each person's birth. There are also censuses that can help you to locate naturalization records. These census facts can lead you to more records, which lead you to more data.

When you look at the Federal Census records you may see things you did not realize or thought were coincidences. Look at the names of families on the page in front and the page behind your ancestors. These are the people who lived near your ancestors, and their lives might have been intertwined. The neighbors might be grown children, in-laws, or a family that you know later married into your ancestor's family. On Ancestry.com there is a link on the transcription page, that you can select to view a blank census form. The link is located under the link to see the record itself. Blank census forms can also be found at: http://www.ancestry.com/download/forms

The questionnaires for each census can be found at:

http://www.census.gov/history/www/through_the_decades/questionnaries

FamilySearch has a page containing links to download blank census forms and census heading forms. The census heading forms combine only the headings of the census forms from 1790-1860, and 1870-1930. The 1940 entry takes you to the wiki page for the 1940 census which has links to the 1940 form. FamilySearch census forms can be found at:

http://familysearch.org/learn/wiki/en/United_States_Census_Forms

Search term: US census blank forms

Among the many forms and research aids and timelines at Family Tree Magazine's website, there are free blank census forms. There is also a checklist that you can download from the website to keep track of all of the census forms that you have for a family group or an individual. That can help you organize your work on this day of census research.

There is a website where you can download Excel spreadsheets of census forms at http://censustools.com. You can download spreadsheets and enter the census data into cells of a preformatted spreadsheet.

Discoveries in the Census

When you have collected a set of censuses for an individual, or a family unit, examine them for interesting data. Looking at the census for Robert Frost in 1910, you can find his children's names and the names of his in-laws. Assuming that his mother-in-law has not remarried, you have found his wife's maiden name. You can collect approximate birthdates for everyone in the family, and their occupations. Viewing the family as a whole can be the key to finding those records that you are having trouble finding.

Keep in mind the census records for the collateral relatives may also yield these information about your direct ancestors.

Some Notes About Naturalization

The Federal Census can give clues that there might be a naturalization record for your ancestor. In the 1870 census there was a column that was checked if the person was a male of age 25 or older and was a citizen. Seeing that column checked for a foreign-born citizen means that he had been naturalized by 1870, which narrows down the years to search for his naturalization record. Remember that there can be errors in the census records; even if the citizen column is not checked, the ancestor may have been a naturalized citizen.

I encountered an unchecked column, and as a result did not look for an ancestor's naturalization record, only to find out later when doing a general search that he had become a naturalized citizen. From that naturalization record, I found his county of birth in Ireland, which was not mentioned in any of the other US records I had gathered for him.

In the 1900, 1910 and 1920 censuses, there were columns for showing an immigrant's citizenship status. One column was for recording the year of immigration. Another column captured the person's naturalization status: the person was an Alien (al); the person had filed his declaration of intent also known as first papers (pa); or he had been naturalized (na). In 1920, there was a column to enter the year of naturalization. Using this data can guide you to an ancestor's immigration records and naturalization records. Just be aware that these years may have been estimates, and the longer after an event, the less accurate a date tends to be.

Other Sources for Census Data
There are online projects that predate the subscription websites where you can view transcribed census information. Even if you find transcribed records on this website, you will want to locate the actual record and view it yourself. As you recall, there is information that may have been incorrectly transcribed, and there may be additional insights to be gathered by the context of the record (e.g. viewing the neighboring families).

Another warning about using these pages is the number of ads on them. Some of the websites require advertisers to fund their efforts, so you may see a search box for a sponsor that takes you away from the website to a subscription one. Be careful where you enter data and where you click on those web pages.

USGenWeb has a census project. Begin at http://usgenweb.org. On the left side of the home page there is a list of states. Click on the link for your state. This is an all-volunteer project, so each state's page may look different. The New York state page has links for census related material on that page; the Massachusetts state page has a dropdown menu that includes an option for the census part of the webpage. Find out which parts of your state have census data, and view the available transcriptions.

CensusFinder is another website that has census transcriptions. The home page is at http://www.censusfinder.com. From the home page use the dropdown menu to select a state. From the state's page you can view which censuses years they have for specific counties.

Census Online is located at http://www.census-online.com. On the home page, click on the Access Online Census Records link to go to a list of states. From there, click on the state, then the county, and the year of the census. Alternately, within the state you can select on the year of the census and then select the county.

Census Substitutes
If you have wondered how to get around the tragic loss of the 1890 Federal Census, there are some things you can use to fill the gap. You can use city directories and state censuses. There are also projects where records have been compiled into an 1890 Census Substitute. Ancestry.com has a landing page allowing you to search city directories, state censuses, voting lists and other records from: http://search.ancestry.com/search/group/1890census.

Learning More
There is always more to learn. There are resources on the web and articles in genealogical publications. Countless introductory books include a chapter on Federal Census research. One of the books that I found useful was Kathleen Hinckley's *Your Guide to the Federal Census* (Betterway Books, 25 Mar 2002). Although there have been several books written about using Ancestry.com, changes are made so often that the books are soon out of date. A good way to keep track of what is happening at both Ancestry.com and FamilySearch is to visit the Ancestry Insider Blog for unofficial, unauthorized, and relevant information, which can be found at: http://www.ancestryinsider.org. Ancestry.com has its own blog about the many facets of the company and developing stories at: http://blogs.ancestry.com/ancestry.

YouTube offers channels for its users to upload videos. Some genealogy videos on YouTube can be informative, or like having private tutorials. Ancestry.com has a YouTube channel, found at: http://www.youtube.com/user/AncestryCom. The videos there keep you informed about what's new at Ancestry.com each month, offer quick tips in the Five Minute Finds series, and present a regular show by the Barefoot Genealogist, Crista Cowan.

FamilySearch also has a YouTube channel. Click on the FamilySearch Playlists to see videos about FamilySearch.org, presentations given at the most recent RootsTech Conference, and other topics of interest. FamilySearch offers videos for beginning in genealogy, including the 5 Minute Genealogy video series with helpful hints, which can be found by entering 5 Minute Genealogy in the YouTube search box. The address of the channel is:
http://www.youtube.com/user/FamilySearch

Explore the resources in the Ancestry.com Learning Center, located at http://learn.ancestry.com. Here you can find more resources about census records, state research guides and short articles about getting started in many areas of genealogical research.

ProQuest has guides for the Ancestry.com Library Edition that are helpful to users located at:
http://proquest.libguides.com/c.php?g=87030&p=559614

Learn About Transcribing Records
The professionals who are hired by the major companies to index U.S. records are usually very competent. Companies hire people who are experts in transcribing and understanding historical forms of writing, called paleography.
Search term: paleography

The organizations that are using volunteers to crowdsource the indexing of records usually assign two people to index the record, and then have one arbitrator designated to resolve resulting differences. This process minimizes the chance of incorrectly transcribing the names that appear on the record, but it is not foolproof.

I recommend that you volunteer to index, perhaps in one of the well-organized FamilySearch Indexing Projects. This will give you practice deciphering old handwriting, and as a side effect you may become more patient with indexing errors. It is hard to interpret some of the names, especially when they are ones with which you are not familiar.

The Census and Oral Interviews

Your older relatives may have information about events that will further your research, and their memories may hold the keys to unlocking genealogical mysteries. I recommend interviewing these people, beginning with the oldest family member first. When interviewing people, you can use the gathered census records to generate talking points and show them to the interviewees. If you can, display the census records on a computer screen so that the writing can be enlarged.

If the people you are interviewing were in the census you are showing them, looking at the record may jog their memories and unleash stories about their neighborhood and childhood. When my late Mother looked at the 1930 census record for her family, she scanned through the names of the neighbors. It was as if she traveled back in time through the census. She fondly remembered the family that lived next to them, recalling that they had a farm in Brooklyn, and raised chickens.

Other Census Schedules

Enumerators collected data beyond what is included in the population schedules. This additional data was collected in supplemental schedules which provide more details of how people lived. For some census years there were Agricultural, Industry, Manufacturing, and Slave schedules. There was a Mortality schedule. There was a Defective, Dependent and Delinquent Classes (DDD) schedule as part of the 1880 Federal Census.

The agricultural schedules record how many animals were owned, and the value of the crops that were farmed. Some of these are available on Ancestry.com.

Mortality schedules were done four times, between 1850 and 1880 (inclusive). Their purpose was to assess the health of the country before vital records required by law in all states. The mortality schedules recorded deaths in the 365 days before the census date. Some mortality schedules are online at Ancestry.com and at FamilySearch, and I have found some at state archives.

To learn more about the other census schedules, go to the U.S. Census Bureau website, described in the next section.

Family Tree Magazine has many excellent resources at their website, http://familytreemagazine.com. Click the Research

Toolkit in the buttons near the top of the page. From there, you can find links to free forms, cheat sheets and other resources. Blank forms are at: http://familytreemagazine.com/info/censusforms. There is a document in those resources called "Where to Find 1880 DDD Supplemental Census Records", which can be found at: http://www.familytreemagazine.com/upload/images/PDF/DDDschedules.pdf

U.S. Census Bureau Information

From the homepage of the U.S. Census Bureau, click on the Genealogy button near the top of the page to see content of interest to genealogists. Alternately, you can use the web address http://www.census.gov/history/www/genealogy (Figure 18). Click on the Genealogy box to view the drop down menu containing links to Decennial Census Records and Other Resources. The Other Resources page contains information about: State Censuses, Nonpopulation Records, Mortality Schedules, and Other Genealogical Sources. This information includes where to find these records. A census image gallery can be found at: http://www.census.gov/history/www/sights_sounds/photos

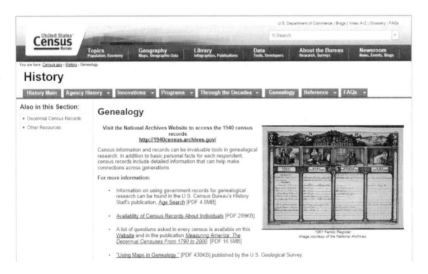

Figure 18. U.S. Census Bureau Genealogy Web Page.

State Censuses

State and territory censuses were usually taken in years between the federal censuses. Using these censuses helps you to create events on your ancestors' timelines. You can google the name of your state and the words "state census" to look for records. Ancestry.com and FamilySearch have put many of the state censuses online.

Search terms: <state name> "state census"

Example: "New York" "state census"

Get Ready for the Next Census Release

The census is taken every ten years, however for privacy reasons there is a delay of 72 years for each census to be released. The 1940 census was released on 2 April 2012. Although it was legal to release it on 1 April, that day was a Sunday, so it was released online Monday morning at the beginning of the business day on the east coast of the United States. The next federal census to be released is the 1950 Federal Census, which can be legally released on April 1, 2022.

Even if the release of the next census is years away, you can begin to get ready for its release. Since censuses are released to everyone at the same time, there will be no index of names when the census is first avalable.

If you cannot wait until there is an index to find your ancestors, you will need to locate the enumeration district (ED) for your ancestors' address, and search the images, one page at a time, to find your ancestors. Searching for an ancestor in a small town or village is usually easier than searching for an ancestor in a large metropolitan area.

Enumeration Districts may change each census year. There are many helpful finding and search aids on the One-Step Webpages by Stephen P. Morse at http://stevemorse.org (Figure 19). Scroll down to the folder entitled US Census (1790-1940), and click on the plus sign next to it to view his census tools. Steve Morse has led a volunteer project that builds databases of EDs by description and automates the discovery of the enumeration district. Since the release of the 1940 census ED Finder, he began working on the 1950 ED Finder.

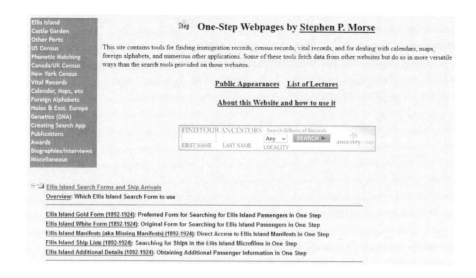

Figure 19. One-Step Webpages by Stephen P. Morse.

Rest assured that the major companies and the volunteer crowdsourcing efforts will begin immediately to create an index. If genealogy remains such a popular pursuit, and the genealogical community's support during the 1940 Federal Census release is an indicator, indexes will be available quickly.

You can always wait for an index rather than research enumeration districts. The wait time might be reasonable. To put things in perspective, it took about 15 years to index the 1880 Federal Census using an offline process. More recently, indexing the 1920 Federal Census took 2 years and making a second index for the 1930 Federal Census was done in 9 months. Using computer-based resources and crowdsourcing, the 132 million names of the 1940 Federal Census were indexed by FamilySearch volunteers in 4 months. The reduction in time is remarkable when we consider that the population, and hence the numbers of names to index, grows with each subsequent census.

More to Do: You in the Census

If you are of an age to have been included in one of the released censuses, remember to find and download those census images.

Recreate the censuses you were counted in that have not been released. Imagine how you would have advanced your research if

your ancestors had done the same. You can find the questionnaires on the U.S. Census Bureau website at:
http://www.census.gov/history/www/through_the_decades/questionnaires/

More to Do: Trace the Collateral Lines
When you have traced a direct line of ancestors back in time to its first appearance in a Federal Census, you can try tracking the collateral branches of the family going forward.

More to Do: Surname Study
Consider gathering data for all the people with a given surname within a geographic area. This is a surname study. Tracking a group of related people gives you a wider net to find out more about your ancestor. You may find evidence of a group migration, or a chain of migrations. When ancestors have common names, you will have a reference to determine if you have located the correct person. The data you collect can be enhanced by including information from other sources, such as city directories and draft records.

Final Thoughts
My suggestion is to hunt for one family line at a time in each day you set aside for census research, and go through the census years in reverse. Collecting a set of sequential censuses is like having an album of snapshots of the lives of an ancestor or a whole family.

Use the checklist you find at Family Tree Magazine, or your own, and see if you can find all members of a family group in each census. You can then expand your search for the state (or in some cases, city) censuses for that family. Record the data in your favorite genealogy program as you go, and you will find the censuses fill in an amazing amount of data like residence addresses, occupations, and approximate dates of birth and marriage and naturalization.

Even if the census is one you have looked at before, look at it again with fresh eyes. Every time I return to a census record I find more information, and form new hypotheses.

If you fail to find a family unit in a particular census, use the timeline, and all the tricks you have learned in this chapter to find them.

When a family member disappears from the family group between censuses that is your cue to search for evidence of life events like marriage, relocation, or even death.

SUNDAY:
Google for Genealogy

There is a lot of content on the web. People are posting family websites that are automatically generated by their family tree software. Historical and genealogical societies are participating in projects to document cemeteries and other landmarks in their local areas. Queries and responses are being posted on message boards.

Using Google or other Internet search engines in your genealogical research is part of an active approach that goes beyond the confines of data services, to find these resources that can further your research. Sunday's activity is to learn to use learn how to structure Google searches with genealogy in mind to locate content on the web about your ancestors. Other Internet search engines will be described in the following chapter, entitled Beyond Sunday.

This chapter introduces you to the essential building blocks of a query, which is how you ask a search engine to look for something. By combining these building blocks, we can ask Google to look for specific information on web pages. Looking at the results of your searches, you can further tailor your queries, and make subsequent searches more effective. The Internet is always changing so you will need to repeat these searches in the future, too.

Google is more than a search engine. Several other Google products that can help you are also discussed in this chapter.

The techniques in this section have been very useful to me in the search for my ancestors. I have discovered posts on message boards and on regional genealogical societies' web sites. I have also found transcriptions of tombstones and wills, and contents of private collections.

The Ground Rules
When we talk about Google searches we are talking about the words, called search terms, which are entered in the box on the Google homepage, http://www.google.com, and pressing the button labeled "Google Search" (Figure 20). The "I'm Feeling Lucky" button next to it takes you to the web page where first result is found. I rarely feel that lucky, and I also want to see the results returned from the search. Google terms are not case sensitive, so you do not have to slow yourself down by spending time hitting the shift key. If you want to put a Google search box at the top of your browser, you can download and install it from: http://www.google.com/toolbar.

Figure 20. Google Home Page.

You will use combinations of search operators, described in this section, with your search terms. The search operators do have to appear in all capital letters, so that Google recognizes them. After you read about an operator, try it. Then try it again within a couple of days. That will help you retain the techniques you learn. Remember to keep track of your searches, so that you can reuse and refine them. I usually open a Word document, and cut-and-paste the search terms as I use them into the document for future reference. There is also a worksheet at the end of the chapter to help structure your searches.

Google can only show results from websites that allow themselves to be indexed. Google cannot go behind the wall of a paid service. Many of the pages we see on commercial databases are not static; they are generated when we send requests. Those pages that are created on the fly cannot be searched by Google.

Operator: AND

When you use the AND operator, Google is told that all results must have all the terms you typed in the search box. In fact, you do not have to use the AND operator; Google understands that all the terms you typed in the search box have to appear on the web pages unless otherwise specified. The terms can appear anywhere on the page, and do not have to be adjacent or in the order in which you typed them.

Operator: OR

Your results will have either or both of the terms that appear on either side of the OR operator. One way to use the OR operator is to look for alternate spellings.

Example: McMahon OR McMann

Operator: "" (exact quote)

The double quotes let you search for an exact word or phrase. This helps you look for a word we would expect to find on a webpage with genealogical information, such as "born". An exact phrase could be a person's name, "William Matier". This operator is good for including place names and key words in your search terms.

The double quotes force Google to use the stop words, which are words that Google usually ignores when it searches (e.g. a, an, the, on, where, how). By forcing Google to use these words, you can look for the title of a book, or a song.

You can combine terms in double quotes to look for combinations of exact terms or words. An example is looking for two names together, such as a husband and wife.

Example: "Joseph McMahon" "Ella Small"

A name and an event can also be combined.

Example: William Matier" "born"

Another use is to search for a name in its usual order, or in the order it appears in a roster

Example: "William Matier" OR "Matier, William"

Specifying both ways that a name can appear is a powerful combination, because we can find the name in records, or in military, church, or jury rosters.

Operator: * (wildcard)

The * is a fill-in-the-blank operator. It is a wildcard for zero or more letters. When I begin research in a place not known to me, I use it to find the county where the city or town resides.

Example: Ames is in * county IA"

Combined with the OR operator, a wildcard can help you find web pages that contain an ancestor's name, with or without a middle name or initial.

Example: "William Matier" OR "William * Matier"

Operator: - (exclude)

Using this operator tells Google which terms to exclude. It is a hyphen, which looks like a minus sign. There can be no space between the hyphen and the keyword you want to exclude. This operator is useful if your searches include a city name that may occur in multiple states. When I search for my ancestors in Manhattan, I want results to be about the borough in New York City, in New York State, not in Kansas.

Example: Manhattan -Kansas

Since this is an operator in Google, take care when you use a hyphenated name, and put the whole name in quotes to ensure the search is for that exact phrase.

Operator: year1..year2

The .. operator is used for a numeric range search. Google searches for numbers on web pages that fall between the range of numbers you specify. The range is inclusive, meaning that it searches for the numbers on both endpoints, too. This operator is useful when searching for a range of years.

Example: "sarah bush" "born" 1700..1800

Operator: ˜ (tilde)

Use the tilde (~) to instruct Google to return results similar to the search term it precedes. There can be no space between the ~ and the term. Although there is no official list of the similar terms, looking in the search results will give you an idea of what terms Google has determined are similar. Using the term ˜genealogy returns results with terms like family history. Similar terms does not include variations in spelling of names.

Examples: mcmahon ~genealogy

mcmahon ~ancestry

Operator: site:

If you have ever found a great web page, and lamented that there was no search box for you to use to find out what other useful pages are on the website, this operator can help. You specify the term you are looking for, and the site you wish to search. If the website allows Google to search its website, this will work. You can specify multiple terms.

Examples: bush site:www.mdgensoc.org

shadrach bush site:www.mdgensoc.org

Operators: inurl: and allinurl:

The inurl: operator is used to limit the search results to those websites that include a specific term in the web address (uniform resource locator (URL)). Do not use a space between the operator and the search term.

If there are multiple words you want to appear in the web addresses of the search results, you can use the operator inurl: in front of each term, or you can use the allinurl: in front of all the terms that should be included. When using the allinurl: operator, spaces can be used to separate the terms that you want to appear in the addresses.

Example: I recalled seeing maps of Cattaraugus County that included names of the land owners on the Painted Hills Genealogy Society webpage, but I could not remember the web address of the Society.

Example: cattaraugus county map inurl:paintedhills

If I knew that painted hills appeared in the address, but did not recall if the words were adjacent to each other, I would use the allinurl: operator. This operator allows spaces between the words, as everything that follows the operator is assumed to be in the address.

Example: cattaraugus county map allinurl: painted hills

Table of Key Operators

A table of the key operators used in Google searches and their definitions is included in Table 2.

Table 2. Google Operators.

OPERATOR	DEFINITION
AND	All specified words must be in results Always implied between search words (do not need it)
OR	Any or all of the words
"word"	Exact search for one word, No synonyms are returned
"word1 word2"	An exact search for these words in specified order
"word1 * word2"	Something can come in the middle of these words (e.g. a middle initial)
-	NOT operator (no space after -) Results cannot include this word
year1..year2	Range of dates to include in results (inclusive)
~	Return results with similar terms Tilde is upper case of key left of 1
site:	Restrict search to specific site/domain (no space after site:)
inurl:	Results will have only the word that appears after the operator in the web page's address
allinurl:	Results will have the words that appears after the operator in the web page's address

Example Series of Searches

When a search returns a million or more results that does not help you, rather it creates more work. You will want to try additional combinations of search terms, in multiple searches, to trim those results and get high quality in what is returned to you. Look at the results for each search and use the information you know about the ancestor to fine tune your next search.

In Table 3 you can see how many results I had on a series of searches. When I used the first and last names of a friend's ancestor as keywords in the Google search box there were over 900,000 results. That is too many for me to reasonably view no matter how good a friend he is, so I began adding additional terms to focus on what I knew about the ancestor. Adding the exact term "Maryland" narrowed things down quite a bit, but there were still too many results. I looked at the family history, and knew that the part of the family I was interested in had migrated to Ohio, so I included the exact search term, "Ohio". This served to narrow down the results, but there were still too many for me to examine in detail. When I looked at these results, I saw another branch of the family had migrated to Pennsylvania. At this point I wanted to focus on only the direct ancestors, so I opted to eliminate those results that contained Pennsylvania. Of course, I will keep in mind what these results yielded about a branch of the family moving to Pennsylvania, and may decide in the future to explore those branches.

Table 3. Shadrach Bush Searches.

Search terms	No. of Results
shadrach bush	915,000
shadrach bush "maryland"	244,000
shadrach bush "maryland" "ohio"	219,000
shadrach bush "maryland" "ohio" -pennsylvania	61,600

I decided to try another approach. After all, Google searches are free. I focused this group of searches on the names of the couple. Table 4 contains examples of the searches I tried, and the number of results for each. Trying "Shadrach Bush" and Sarah (without Sarah being an exact term) yielded a reasonable number of results. I was able to check through this list rapidly. Among these results were a transcription of Shadrach Bush, Jr.'s will, queries about the Bush family on the Maryland Genealogical Society's website, an assessment of 1783 Baltimore County from the Maryland State Archives and a FindAGrave memorial. When I used the exact phrase "Sarah Osborne" instead of the term Sarah, I had very few results, but those results were of high quality. Thinking that there might be records with a middle name, or middle initial for Sarah, I inserted a wildcard in the middle of her name. Remember that the double quotes tell Google to search for an exact phrase, and that the wildcard can be zero or more characters. The two spaces around the wildcard, which probably explained the reduced number of results. In all the records I have seen for Sarah Osborne, none has the included a middle name or middle initial.

I had come across different spellings of Shadrack, so I tried some searches that captured the variations. Using a wildcard for the last letter opened up a large range of possibilities, and produced far too many results to sift through. You can see how selecting only the two variations of spelling the first name, with the OR operator, would cut down on that number of results. By using the whole names as exact phrases, the number of results is cut down significantly. As you look at my examples, you can probably think of several other variations, combinations, and limiting terms that could be used to produce high quality search results. One would be to use "Osborn" so that my search results contain variations of the surname with and without the e on the end.

Table 4. Shadrach Bush Searches.

Search terms	No. of Results
"shadrach bush" sarah	186
"shadrach bush" "sarah osborne"	3
"shadrach bush" "sarah * osborne"	1
shadrac* bush	24,700,000
shadrach OR shadrack bush	1,590,000
"shadrach bush" OR "shadrack bush"	989

Start your searches using general keywords and add more specific terms in your subsequent searches. More specific searches will include place names, alternate spelling of names, and types of events (e.g. born, died). Look at the results from each search and use them to refine your search terms. Exclude the terms you see in the results that contain irrelevant information. Try different combinations in your searches, adding and deleting terms as you go. Keep track of the searches you try, and try them again at a later date.

There is no one exact search that will find everything pertaining to an ancestor. Instead, have a set of fine-tuned searches that cover aspects of the ancestor's life.

Record where you find data. Remember that you will probably want an electronic copy of the web page you find. You can save it, or print it to a portable document format (pdf) document with a product like pdf995. When you use pdf995, the web address is printed along with the document, making it easier to cite the source.

If your ancestor has a common name, or the name of a common item, your searches will need more structure. If anyone in the family unit has an unusual name search for that person. Remember to employ other operators and search terms that may be useful in eliminating the unwanted results, such as locations and ranges of years.

Now that you understand how to use the operators and the keywords together, there is another way to build your searches. Google offers an Advanced Search feature, which appears at the right side of a page of search results from the drop down settings (gear) menu as shown in Figure 21, or you can navigate directly to http://www.google.com/advanced_search.

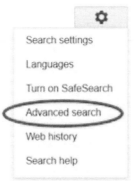

Figure 21. Google Advanced Search Option.

The Advanced Search webpage (Figure 22) guides you through the options you just learned, and you can enter the words you want to be included or excluded in the results, which exact phrases you want to appear, which numeric ranges, and other options about the language, region or timeliness of the webpages.

Figure 22. Google Advanced Search Page.

Google Alerts

When you have built a good set of searches, you will want to try them again a future date to find new content that has been added to the Internet. That is where Google Alerts can help. Google Alerts will automate your searches, and e-mail you the results as often as you have requested they be sent.

You need a Google account to use Google Alerts. If you have Gmail, then you already have an account. If you do not have an account, you can sign up at: http:// www.google.com/accounts.

To set up the alerts, go to http://www.google.com/alerts. Type in your search query, as shown in Figure 23. On the right side of the page you will see a preview of the results. The main information you will select on this page is how often you want the results sent, the quality of the results, and the e-mail address to which you want Google to send the results.

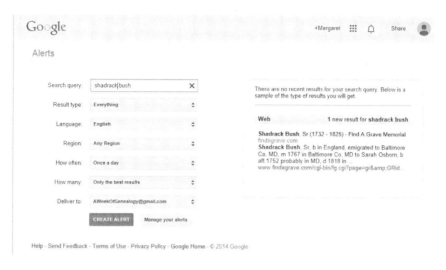

Figure 23. Google Alerts Page.

Learning More

This book has covered search strategies using key operators. These are the ones that I use in my research, but there are others you might find useful. When you are ready to investigate more of the operators, use the search terms below.

Search terms: Google operators

Google cheat sheets

Finding Missing Web Pages: Google Cache

When you look at the results page and see the snippet from a promising webpage, there is nothing more disheartening than clicking on the link and seeing the words "Page Not Found". When that happens, all is not lost! There are a couple of techniques to locate a version of the page that was saved when it was available on the web.

Look for the web address that appears in the second line of the search result snippet. There is a green downward-facing arrow at the end of it. Left click the arrow, and a pop-up box appears (Figure 24). Select Cached, and you will see a view of the page that was captured by Google (Figure 25). This page is not alive as it was on the original website, so the links may not work. However, you can hover your mouse over the links, copy them, and paste them into the Google search box and repeat the process to find other Cached web pages.

Figure 24. Drop Down Menu with Cache Option.

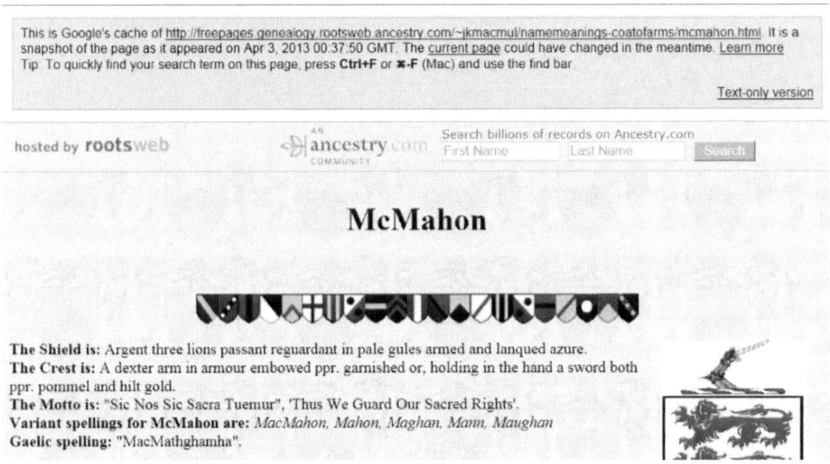

Figure 25. Cached Web Page.

Note: The details of finding the option for viewing the cached page seems to change every time I give a presentation about Google. In the past, the link for the cached copy has appeared next to the web address. In the pop-up box, I have seen the terms: Cached, Similar, Share.

Finding Missing Web Pages: The WayBack Machine
You can use the WayBack Machine at the Internet Archives to locate a copy of the web page if it has been stored. Enter the

webpage's address in the WayBack machine box on the Internet Archive homepage at http://archive.org (Figure 26). If the WayBack Machine has stored a copy of the web page, it will display a timeline with dates of when the web page was captured and allow you to select which version of the page you want to view.

Figure 26. The Internet Archive Home Page.

To illustrate the use of the WayBack Machine, I entered the web address for my faculty page at the U.S. Naval Academy, www.cs.usna.edu/~mmmcmahn (Figure 27).

Figure 27. WayBack Machine Example.

When I clicked on the "Take Me Back" button, I was presented with a timeline of the crawls the WayBack Machine made through the website (Figure 28).

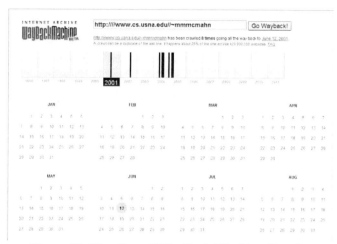

Figure 28. Timeline of WayBack Machine Crawls.

I selected the first year where the web page was crawled, which was in 2001. It was crawled on 12 June 2001. I clicked on that day in the calendar, and can see what my faculty page looked like, including the courses I was teaching that semester (Figure 29). The links are active on this page, although when I clicked on a link in the "Current Courses" section, it was a Forbidden page
. That is because the materials for the courses were not accessible to the outside world; they were only visible to a computer connected to the school's network.

Figure 29. The Stored Web Page.

Google Books

Although this day only covers Google searches, I recommend that you investigate some other Google Products. Search for your ancestors' names in the books digitized by Google using Google Books at http://books.google.com (Figure 30). In addition to looking for ancestors, consider looking for county and local histories which can be rich in useful details. There are also genealogies, and genealogical journals on Google Books. Some results gave books that can be downloaded in pdf or eBook form, while others results are only snippets of books, or have limited pages available for viewing. Use Google search operators, or use the Advanced Search, but be aware that ~ (tilde) operator is not supported. Instead, search separately for the terms: genealogy, family, history.

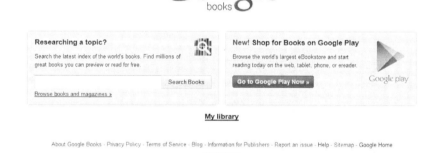

Figure 30. Google Books Home Page.

While finding books that can be downloaded in electronic format is preferable, snippets of books can still be useful. Look for a link to help you find the book in WorldCat where you can locate for libraries that have copies of the book. Your local library might be able to arrange an interlibrary loan or request photocopies of relevant pages. There are also links with buying options.

Google Images

Try using Google Images at http://images.google.com to search for ancestors (Figure 31), and locations. You can enter the same search terms that you would when looking for ancestors.

Figure 31. Google Images Home Page.

Another interesting feature of Google Images is that you can use an image to search the web for similar images (Figure 31). This is done by selecting the camera icon in the search box. You can choose to paste URL (web address) of the image, or upload an image from your computer (Figure 32). This type of search works best when keywords are also added.

Figure 32. Searching by Image.

Google Videos

Google Videos at http://videos.google.com (Figure 33) can be used to locate tours of ancestral locations, genealogy classes, and how-to videos. Google purchased YouTube in 2006. YouTube is a mammoth free video hosting service, so it is not surprising that most of the results are from YouTube. YouTube allows users to upload content, and to have their own channels, for free. One interesting channel is the 5 Minute Genealogy video series at http://www.youtube.com/user/FamilySearch. Another channel that may be useful to you is the Ancestry.com channel, found at http://www.youtube.com/user/Ancestrycom, where you can find helpful webinars, how-to, and the Barefoot Genealogist videos.

Figure 33. Google Videos Home Page.

Google Translate

Google Translate translates text, websites and documents from one language to another. It is found at http://translate.google.com (Figure 34). As of this writing, eighty languages are supported.

When text is entered in the left box, shown in Figure 34, Google attempts to automatically detect the text's language. Alternately, you can select the language. When a web page address is entered in the left box, you can translate the text on the page from its original language to another. There is an option to upload a document for translation.

Google Translate can also be useful when sending an e-mail or letter requesting information in a language with which you are not familiar.

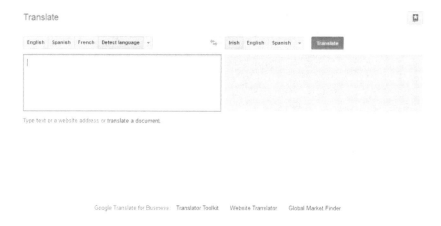

Figure 34. Google Translate Home Page.

There is a legend that during the Cold War attempts were made to use computers to translate text from one language to another. The ultimate test is to translate text from one language to another, then translate it back to the original language. If the resulting message is the same as the beginning one, then the whole process is verified. A computer was asked to translate the English phrase "The spirit was willing, but the flesh was weak" to Russian, then back to English. Unfortunately, the literal translation resulting from the process was, "the vodka was good, but the meat was rotten."

Be aware that if you enter idiomatic or complicated text, you will receive a best effort rather than a definitive translation. A human is still required for correctness.

If you use webpages in many languages, consider using Google's own browser, Google Chrome. Google Chrome has an automatic translator built into it. The Chrome browser can be downloaded from https://www.google.com/chrome/browser. By selecting the Translate icon, you can view a translated version of the webpage you are viewing.

Google Maps

Google Maps at http://maps.google.com can be used to locate family homes, neighborhoods, schools and places of worship near your ancestors (Figure 35). You have the option to switch to satellite view of the area. By using the Directions feature you can also calculate routes that ancestors took. For example, when you read about a route taken by a funeral procession, you can recreate the route and visualize it on Google Maps.

Google Earth

Download Google Earth from http://earth.google.com to visualize places in your genealogy. Google Earth will allow you to use different maps for your coordinates, and includes a way for you to import historical maps and overlay addresses or coordinates on them.

Figure 35. Google Maps Home Page.

Google in Other Countries

Google has country-specific search pages, which offer a localized version of Google. In multi-lingual countries, there is an option under the search box to change the language in which the Google text appears.

To use a country-specific Google page, you substitute the country's top level domain for the "com" at the end of the web address. For example, the web specific Google address for Ireland http://www.google.ie brings you to the Google Ireland specific search page shown in Figure 36.

A full list of Google country codes and top level domains, and their associated languages, can be found at:
https://www.distilled.net/blog/uncategorized/google-cctlds-and-associated-languages-codes-reference-sheet/

Figure 36. Google Ireland Search Page.

Google searches and returns results that are country-centric to the Google page you searched from. It prioritizes the results based on the country of the Google search page that is used. When researching in another country, give their google page a try.

You can force Google to display only the results from web servers in a given country by using a url parameter. After you have searched for the term(s) append to the web address
&cr=countryXX
where XX is the 2 letter identifier for a country, which is the same as its country code top-level domain. Examples: US for the United States, UK for the United Kingdom, and IE for Ireland.

Example: Search for clare, then append the expression &cr=countryIE to the url. The results will be only those located in Ireland.

Google Doodles

On special occasions, there will be a special image or interactive games on the Google Home Page, above the search box. You can view old Google Doodles at http://doodles.google.com.

Google Worksheet
While you are reading this book, and thinking about the types of searches, the best thing to do is to take some notes about the searches you will try using your own ancestors' data.

Use a name "firstName * lastName"

_____

Use a name with last name first

_____

List a location (city or state)

_____

List a location to ignore (if applicable)

_____

Include a life event (if applicable)

_____

Link two names together in your search

_____

Look for a range of years in the results

_____

Try searches combining these terms

_____

BEYOND SUNDAY:
More Internet Searching

In this chapter, we will look at different search engines: Mocavo, a search engine designed for genealogy that also has content; Dogpile; Yippy!; and Gigablast. These search engines are hunting on the Internet, just as Google does, but use different algorithms when searching and different formats to present the search results. We will also look at a computational engine Wolfram|Alpha. These are interesting tools to complement your use of Google, or you may decide to make them your primary tools.

Search Engine: Mocavo
Mocavo was launched on 16 March 2011, by Cliff Shaw who was the creator of the website GenCircles.com. It is billed as the "World's Largest Free Genealogy Search Engine". Mocavo differentiates itself from other Internet search engines by being built with genealogy in mind, and also by being a content provider. There are three levels of membership: Basic (free account), Silver, and Gold. Mocavo is located at: http://www.mocavo.com

As a search engine, Mocavo searches: genealogy message boards, family trees, state and local historical societies, the Library of Congress, the National Archives and Records Administration, Ellis Island, Find A Grave, the Internet Archive, U.S. state archives, individuals' genealogy sites, and genealogy blogs. You have to create a free account to use the search engine.

On 23 June 2014, during the writing of this book, FindMyPast announced that it had purchased Mocavo. They promised that the currently free content will remain free to access at the individual database level. They have also made a commitment to making full indexes to all the Federal Censuses available for free at Mocavo. However, it is reasonable to expect changes in the way that the site appears, and functions.

As a content provider, Mocavo claims to be adding more than 1,000 new Datasets online every day. Searching an individual Dataset is free, but searching across all the datasets requires a paid membership.

After you login, you can select Search to see the web page shown in Figure 37. Search will show results, and results shows snippets, and select "Show Preview". Basic members with free accounts cannot view details of the Datasets from this search results page, and will have to search individual Datasets to see results. Use the filters on the left of the page to narrow down the results.

I searched for my ancestor, Arthur Gilroy, including the keyword Brooklyn. The search results are shown in Figure 38.

Clicking a link on the Search Page took me to the snippet of the Dataset where my ancestor's name appears (Figure 39). This may be enough to tell me that this is not a record for my ancestor. However, a basic member with a free account needs to go to the specific Dataset web page to search that Dataset. With a free Basic

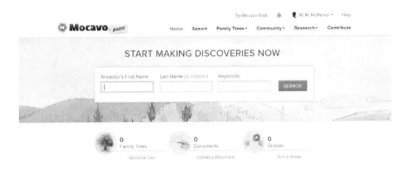

Figure 37. Mocavo Search Page.

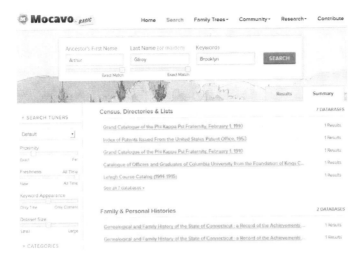

Figure 38. Mocavo Search Results for Arthur Gilroy.

membership, when I clicked on the link, I was offered an option to pay for a type of membership that will allow me to go from the search results page to the individual Datasets. Since I cannot click on the link and be taken to the search page for this Dataset, I will have to locate it a different way.

Figure 39. Mocavo Search Results for Arthur Gilroy (details).

To locate Datasets, you can browse the Records by selecting Research then Records, Books and Datasets, or using the web address http://www.mocavo.com/records. From the Browse web page you can browse content by category (Figure 40) or location (Figure 41). Mocavo also offers the option to search by date. You will need to navigate through these links, to locate the Dataset's web page where you can search for your ancestor.

Another approach is to find the web page for the Dataset by using Google. Google cannot look inside the Dataset to find your ancestors, but can locate the search page for the Dataset. This approach is faster than browsing to get to the webpage for the Dataset. In the search results, note the title of the Dataset, and use the whole title, or keywords, in your Google search.

Example search terms:

connecticut achievements site:mocavo.com

Mocavo's United States Census index census search page (Figure 42) can be found at:

http://www.mocavo.com/1790-1940-United-States-Census/126199

Browse by Category

BMD

| Baptism | Birth | Burial | Christening | Death |
| Divorce | Marriage | | | |

DIRECTORIES

| City or Area | Organizational | Professional |

DOCUMENTS & RECORDS

| Bank & Insurance | Criminal & Court | Government | Immigration | Land |
| Tax | Wills & Estates | | | |

HISTORIES

Church	City	County	Ethnic Group	Family & Biographies
Local or Place	Military	Native American	Royalty	Society & Organization
State				

MILITARY

| Casualties | Draft | Enlistment | Pensions | Service |
| Soldiers, Veterans, Pri. | | | | |

NEWSPAPERS

YEARBOOKS

| College | High School | Navy Cruisebooks | Other |

OTHER

Figure 40. Mocavo Browse by Category.

Browse by Location

AUSTRALIA

CANADA

Alberta	British Columbia	Canada	Manitoba	New Brunswick
Newfoundland & Labr.	Northwest Territories	Nova Scotia	Nunavut	Ontario
Prince Edward Island	Quebec	Saskatchewan	Yukon	

EUROPE

FRANCE

GERMANY

IRELAND

ITALY

NEW ZEALAND

NORTHERN IRELAND

UNITED KINGDOM

| British Indian Ocean T. | England | Great Britain | Isle of Man | Scotland |
| United Kingdom | Wales | | | |

UNITED STATES

REGIONS

Figure 41. Mocavo Browse by Location.

Figure 42. Mocavo Census Index Search Page.

Mocavo allows its community members to upload content. There are family trees, historical documents, and photos. The community has surname groups. There is a free service to scan documents and include them in datasets, but you will have to pay to have the original documents returned to you. You can create or upload family trees to Mocavo.

My personal experience with Mocavo has been mixed. For me, the search engine has not exceeded what I can accomplish with well-crafted Google searches. However, the content part has yielded some interesting twentieth-century publications, like yearbooks and other school publications.

To learn more about Mocavo, you can go to the Mocavo Learning Center at http://learn.mocavo.com. For more Tips and Tricks of Mocavo, go to http://learn.mocavo.com/category/tips-and-tricks.

Search Engine: YAHOO!
Yahoo was launched on 1 March 1 1995. As of January 2014, it is the second largest internet search engine having a 5.45% of the query volume compared to Google's 71.36%. Originally it contained a searchable index of pages, but since 2009, Microsoft's Bing has powered Yahoo search. When you go to the webpage at http://www.yahoo.com you are greeted with an interface geared to delivering content. It includes a panel that allows access to Yahoo mail and Flickr among other services (Figure 43).

Figure 43. YAHOO! Home Page.

Search Engine: Dogpile

Dogpile uses a Metasearch algorithm, delivering results from Google and Yahoo! Dogpile began in November 1996 and can be found at: http://www.dogpile.com (Figure 44). You can search for webpages, images, audio, news, white pages, and yellow pages.

The Boolean operators can be used in searches, but they only work from the advanced search page (Figure 45).

The order of your search terms in important, so put them in order of importance carefully. Type your search terms in the search box, and click "Fetch It!". Ads and Web Results are presented on the results page (Figure 46).

You can then use the "Are you looking for?" links on the left side of the webpage that Dogpile thinks will further your search. Recent searches also appear on the left side of the search results page.

I was able to search for multiple exact phrases, such as my grandparents' names, using double quotes ("") around each name in the search box.

Example: "Joseph McMahon" "Ella Small"

Dogpile Tricks of the Trade can be found at: http://www.dogpile.com/support/tips

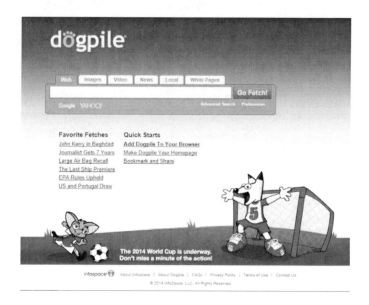

Figure 44. Dogpile Home Page.

Figure 45. Dogpile Advanced Search Page.

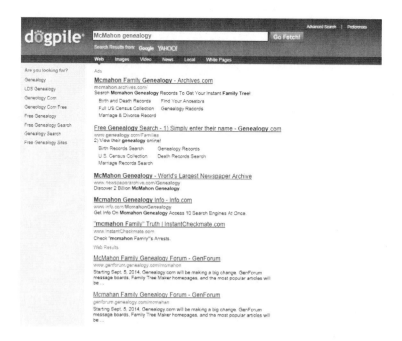

Figure 46. Dogpile Example Search Results.

Clustering Engine: Yippy!

Yippy! provides a clustering web metasearch. Yippy! is at http://yippy.com (Figure 47) and was formerly Clusty. It has a policy of being family friendly. Yippy! attempts to categorize your results and group them into clusters. It is not case sensitive and supports the search operators: AND, OR, NOT, " ", and site:.

On the home page, you can restrict your search by selecting the source: web, news, images, yuckout, football, Wikipedia, Shakespeare, Ben Franklin, Wii, shopping, government, jobs, and blogs. Yuckout is intended to provide a child-friendly search experience by filtering out yucky results.

The search results appear in categories on the left side of the page that allow you to see how the results are grouped. To gain insight into the results, there are tabs for: cloud, source, sites (top level domains), and time. You can also search to find terms within the results. The search results page has a link labeled "advanced" for the advanced search page. The advanced search provides options to insert your query and to select the host, language, filetype, and number of results.

© 2009-2014 Yippy, Inc. *Y* All Rights Reserved. Ticker Symbol **(OTC PINK:YIPI)**

Figure 47. Yippy! Home Page.

Search Engine: Gigablast

Gigablast was founded in 2000 by Matt Wells, with an emphasis on searching performance and continuous updating of its search index. It allows you to view a cached version of a web page in the results, if the website permits Gigablast to cache the pages on the website.

Questions can also be entered into the search box (Figure 48). An advanced search is also available. Syntax help can be found at: http://www.gigablast.com/help.html.

Figure 48. Gigablast Search Engine.

Computational Knowledge Engine: Wolfram|Alpha

Wolfram|Alpha is a computational knowledge engine, shown in Figure 49. It can be used to compute answers and provide knowledge. It can also gather data and present the comparisons. Enter your terms and press the compute button (orange square).

Figure 49. Wolfram|Alpha Home Page.

The simplest use of Wolfram|Alpha is to retrieve data about a name, by entering the name in the input field.

Example Wolfram|Alpha Input: Michael
When I entered the name Michael, and pressed the compute button, Wolfram Alpha informed me of the assumptions it made and its interpretation of my input (Figure 50). It returned Information for US Births, where I learned that Michael is 7th most popular male name; the History for US Births with a graph showing me that Michael appears to have been most popular in the late 1960s; the current age distribution of Michaels in the US; the alternate versions of the name; notable people named Michael; and the etymology of the name.

Figure 50. Wolfram|Alpha Example Results.

When the engine runs out of its allotted time to return data, there is an option at the bottom of the results page labeled "Try again with additional computation time".

Example Wolfram|Alpha Input: Surnames
I tried a basic search with several surnames. There were results for the more common surnames, like McMahon, while the less frequent Tingue surname could not be interpreted as input.

Example Wolfram|Alpha Input: 1880 US Census

When I input the terms: 1880 us census, Wolfram|Alpha returned the population history, and offered me the option to have population predictions performed (Figure 51).

The results included a long-term population history, and the population of major cities in 1880.

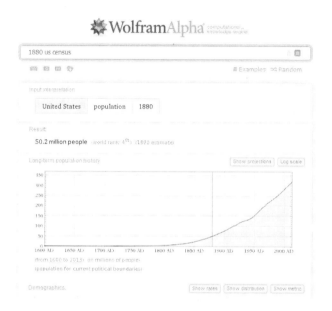

Figure 51. Wolfram|Alpha 1880 Census Search Results.

Example Wolfram|Alpha Input: New York vs Maryland

When I asked Wolfram|Alpha to compare New York and Maryland, it told me that it had assumed New York was a state, and gave me the option to use New York as a city instead.

The results include comparisons of information about the population demographics, education, income, crime statistics, and more (Figure 52).

Hint: to save this data, take a screenshot, or print to a pdf. Saving the page from the browser will not save the results.

With a subscription, Wolfram|Alpha will process image, data, or a file that you upload.

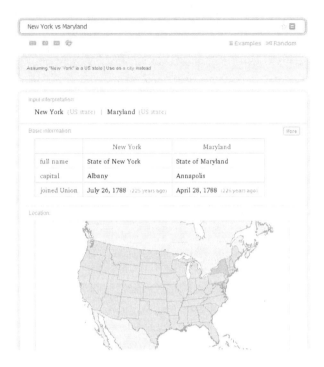

Figure 52. Wolfram|Alpha New York vs Maryland Results.

Investigate the examples to find out the types of questions you can ask: http://www.wolframalpha.com/examples and take a tour at http://www.wolframalpha.com/tour/what-is-wolframalpha.html.

Evaluating a Search Engine

There are other search engines available. You need to be able to evaluate them for yourself. Search for how-to documentation and read about what search operators you can use. Use some of the searches you have developed for Google in the search engine.

Search terms: <name of search engine> operators

Search terms: <name of search engine> how to

There are ways to learn more about the search engines, like Google's Official Blog at http://googleblog.blogspot.com. How Search Engines Work at http://www.learnthenet.com/animated-internet/how-search-engines-work/index.php, and Search Engine Watch at http://searchenginewatch.com/industry.

The Beaufort Library University of South Caroline (USC) has a Bare Bones Basic Tutorial on Searching the Web that includes information about using many specific search engines at: www.sc.edu/beaufort/library/pages/bones/bones.shtml.

ONLINE SAFETY

Much of my genealogy work is done online. If you are reading this book, the chances are you currently use or are thinking of using online resources. This chapter presents a few ideas about staying safe in cyberspace.

Passwords

While you have always heard about the importance of choosing strong passwords, be sure you understand what that means.

There are many automated tools that can be used to figure out, or crack, passwords. Anyone possessing your password can access accounts you have at subscription websites, on social media websites, or on websites that require registration to use. People do not have to be geniuses to use these cracking tools; they are freely available to anyone who is unscrupulous enough to download them from the Internet and use them. These folks may not be targeting one specific user, but looking for any easy-to-crack password on a particular website.

A strong password is one that is not easily cracked by the available tools or simply guessed. Good passwords contain combinations of upper case and lower case letters, numbers, and symbols.

Do not use passwords that are names or words that appear in a dictionary.

Do not use the same password for all your accounts. Of course, protect your passwords from others, and do not share them. No legitimate representative of a company or a bank should ever ask for your password to access your account. If they do, suggest that they reset the password on their end. When they are done helping you, then you can change it to something only you know. Asking someone to reset a password is also a good test to see if they are actually an authorized representative of the company or bank that they claim to be.

Microsoft has tips to choose a strong password at:

http://windows.microsoft.com/en-us/windows-vista/tips-for-creating-a-strong-password

You can test something similar to your password (do not type in your real password!) at https://howsecureismypassword.net.

Know About Social Engineering

Social engineering is a technique used by people to gather information and details about other people or organizations, so that they can masquerade as someone they are not. The purpose of social engineering may be to gain access to a computer, a building, or access to another individual's bank account.

Remember that you do not know the people that you "meet" on the Internet.

Genealogists tend to be generous and sharing, but you need to stay alert and aware. At best, the people you have contact with online are cousins you do not know yet. Look to build your confidence that they are who they say they are during exchanges of information about deceased people at first, not the living. It is important to remember that living relative's data has to be protected online as well; be careful what you post about yourself and family members online.

Viruses, Worms, and Malware

When we click on a link in an e-mail message or on a web page, or open an e-mail attachment, malicious software (malware) capable of harming your computer or changing how it works can come to you.

Anyone who connects a computer to the Internet needs to have an anti-virus (AV) software product installed on that computer.

That AV software needs to be from a reputable company; some of the ads that offer software to scan and fix your computer may actually download malicious software! It is not enough to purchase the AV software, or install it; users need to keep the software updated. Those updates contain information about detecting the newest threats that have been found, and are essential to helping protect your computer. While they are limited to protecting you from the known threats, this goes a long way to keeping your machine uninfected or undamaged by malware.

When you set up the AV software, you are usually prompted to allow the software to schedule regular automated scans of your computer. Be sure to scan regularly.

Many of the websites that offer advertising do not screen the advertisers or check out the destination websites where the links in the advertisements lead. Beware of what links you choose to click.

Be a Cautious User: Links and E-mail Attachments
There are several things you can do to keep your computer safe. Do not open e-mails sent by people you do not know. Usually, moving your mouse over (hovering over) the sender's name without clicking on it will show the e-mail address of the sender. Look at the sender's e-mail address, especially the part of the address after the @ symbol, which is the domain name. If the address has looks like gibberish, it is probably from a malicious user. Unfortunately most of the website domain names that are being registered are for malicious users who choose a random collection of symbols or odd words strung together as the names.

If you have clicked on a link that made you uncertain, or something odd happens on your computer after visiting a web page, run a scan for malware.

Some malware comes as email attachments. When the attachments are open, the malware executes causing changes to a computer and installs itself. The installed malware might make the computer a zombie or bot in a botnet. This malware can exist on your computer without your knowledge and participate in mailing spam e-mails, or be involved in a distributed denial of service (DDoS) attack. There is a type of malware called ransomware that encrypts all the data on your hard drive, requiring you to pay a ransom to decrypt it.

Unless you are sure about the contents of an attachment do not open it. Knowing the sender is not enough to trust the attachment; the sender's computer could be infected and the sender unaware that the message was sent. It is always fine to reply to a message and ask what it contains, or make a phone call. An ounce of prevention is truly worth a pound of cure in these circumstances.

Freeware and Shareware
Be cautious of the free software that you download from the Internet. Your AV software will scan the downloaded program, but it can only recognize previously identified malware. Make sure that the program you are downloading is legitimate, and also verify that you are downloading it from a reputable website. If you download a legitimate program from a disreputable website, you may be downloading malware that will install itself.

Backups
Be prepared for bad things that might happen. The bad things include your computer crashing, or destruction of the computer, or accidental deletion of data. To be prepared, you need to back up your data. Your options are to back up the data by storing a copy in the cloud or on an external drive.

When data is stored in the cloud, it is kept on a server that is attached to the Internet. Free accounts may be acceptable for smaller amounts of data, or you may decide to pay an annual fee. If you do use cloud storage, I recommend using a service that allows you to encrypt the data before it is transmitted. If you choose an automatic backup, be sure you know which folders on your computer are being backed up.

Backups should be in a separate location, which is a big argument for putting family trees and supporting data on a trusted genealogy website. The downside is that people may use the material and present it as their own.

Check the Website
URLQuery is a webpage where you can check that the contents of a webpage are not malicious without visiting it (Figure 53). It analyzes the items found at the webpage specified by the address and detects web-based malware. The URLQuery is located at

http://urlquery.net. Enter the address of the page you want to check out in the Profile URL box and press GO!. This website will load the whole web page and scan it, and report if the page has malicious elements.

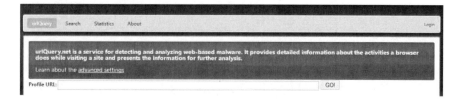

Figure 53. URLQuery Webpage.

Being an educated and aware Internet user will help you to keep yourself and your computer safe.

CONCLUDING THOUGHTS

Thank you for reading this book and spending a weekend of genealogy with me.

In a sense, this book could have been titled, Weekends of Genealogy, as I hope you spend many weekend days searching for and finding census records, and that Google searches become a regular part of your online life. These activities will keep you moving on your quest to learn more about your family.

Keep learning. There are links throughout the book to more resources. Go to see speakers, read magazines, check out websites, and speak to other genealogists. There is always more to learn, and experiencing a different perspective can make things seem clearer.

For my tutorials, upcoming speaking engagements, and to sign up for the mailing list, visit http://aweekofgenealogy.com. If you are interested in more frequent tips, resources and links, Like the Facebook page for *A Weekend of Genealogy* and *A Week of Genealogy*: https://www.facebook.com/AWeekofGenealogy.

I would like to hear about your search tips and your successes. You can reach me by e-mail at: aweekofgenealogy@gmail.com.

ABOUT THE AUTHOR

Margaret M. McMahon is the hockey-playing genealogist. She has a PhD in Computer Science and Engineering, and with the advent of parenthood, she turned her technical talents to researching her family's genealogy. She has over thirty years of engineering experience, including being a college and graduate school professor. She is an experienced presenter at national and international technical conferences.

Dr. McMahon has been an invited speaker at several branches of her local Public Library and genealogical societies in the Washington DC area.

She is a volunteer for the Navy Marine Corps Relief Society, and a member of the Anne Arundel Genealogical Society, and the Society of the Naval Treaty. Her interests include playing and coaching ice hockey and needlework.

Carolyn Edison